INTRODUCING
ISSUES WITH
OPPOSING
VIEWPOINTS®

Drug Legalization

Noël Merino, *Book Editor*

GREENHAVEN PRESS
A part of Gale, Cengage Learning

GALE
CENGAGE Learning·

Detroit • New York • San Francisco • New Haven, Conn • Waterville, Maine • London

Elizabeth Des Chenes, *Director, Content Strategy*
Cynthia Sanner, *Publisher*
Douglas Dentino, *Manager, New Product*

For more information, contact:
Greenhaven Press
27500 Drake Rd.
Farmington Hills, MI 48331-3535
Or you can visit our Internet site at gale.cengage.com

For product information and technology assistance, contact us at

Gale Customer Support, 1-800-877-4253
For permission to use material from this text or product, submit all requests online at
www.cengage.com/permissions

Further permissions questions can be e-mailed to permissionrequest@cengage.com

Articles in Greenhaven Press anthologies are often edited for length to meet page require-ments. In addition, original titles of these works are changed to clearly present the main thesis and to explicitly indicate the author's opinion. Every effort is made to ensure that Greenhaven Press accurately reflects the original intent of the authors. Every effort has been made to trace the owners of copyrighted material.

Cover image © Yellowj/Shutterstock.com.

LIBRARY OF CONGRESS CATALOGING-IN-PUBLICATION DATA

Drug legalization / Noël Merino, book editor.
    pages cm. -- (Introducing issues with opposing viewpoints)
Includes bibliographical references and index.
Audience: Age 14-18.
Audience: Grades 9 to 12.
ISBN 978-0-7377-6275-4 (hardcover)
1. Drug legalization--United States--Juvenile literature. 2. Drug control--United States--Juvenile literature. 3. Drug legalization--Juvenile literature. 4. Drug control--Juvenile literature. I. Merino, Noël.
  HV5825.D77667 2013
  362.29'156--dc23
                                                                                            2013002509

Printed in the United States of America
1 2 3 4 5 6 7 16 15 14 13 12

Contents

Chapter 3: How Should Public Policy on Drugs Be Reformed?

Foreword

Indulging in a wide spectrum of ideas, beliefs, and perspectives is a critical cornerstone of democracy. After all, it is often debates over differences of opinion, such as whether to legalize abortion, how to treat prisoners, or when to enact the death penalty, that shape our society and drive it forward. Such diversity of thought is frequently regarded as the hallmark of a healthy and civilized culture. As the Reverend Clifford Schutjer of the First Congregational Church in Mansfield, Ohio, declared in a 2001 sermon, "Surrounding oneself with only like-minded people, restricting what we listen to or read only to what we find agreeable is irresponsible. Refusing to entertain doubts once we make up our minds is a subtle but deadly form of arrogance." With this advice in mind, Introducing Issues with Opposing Viewpoints books aim to open readers' minds to the critically divergent views that comprise our world's most important debates.

Introducing Issues with Opposing Viewpoints simplifies for students the enormous and often overwhelming mass of material now available via print and electronic media. Collected in every volume is an array of opinions that captures the essence of a particular controversy or topic. Introducing Issues with Opposing Viewpoints books embody the spirit of nineteenth-century journalist Charles A. Dana's axiom: "Fight for your opinions, but do not believe that they contain the whole truth, or the only truth." Absorbing such contrasting opinions teaches students to analyze the strength of an argument and compare it to its opposition. From this process readers can inform and strengthen their own opinions, or be exposed to new information that will change their minds. Introducing Issues with Opposing Viewpoints is a mosaic of different voices. The authors are statesmen, pundits, academics, journalists, corporations, and ordinary people who have felt compelled to share their experiences and ideas in a public forum. Their words have been collected from newspapers, journals, books, speeches, interviews, and the Internet, the fastest growing body of opinionated material in the world.

Introducing Issues with Opposing Viewpoints shares many of the well-known features of its critically acclaimed parent series, Opposing Viewpoints. The articles are presented in a pro/con format, allowing readers to absorb divergent perspectives side by side. Active reading questions preface each viewpoint, requiring the student to approach the material thoughtfully and carefully. Useful charts, graphs, and cartoons supplement each article. A thorough introduction provides readers with crucial background on an issue. An annotated bibliography points the reader toward articles, books, and websites that contain additional information on the topic. An appendix of organizations to contact contains a wide variety of charities, nonprofit organizations, political groups, and private enterprises that each hold a position on the issue at hand. Finally, a comprehensive index allows readers to locate content quickly and efficiently.

Introducing Issues with Opposing Viewpoints is also significantly different from Opposing Viewpoints. As the series title implies, its presentation will help introduce students to the concept of opposing viewpoints and learn to use this material to aid in critical writing and debate. The series' four-color, accessible format makes the books attractive and inviting to readers of all levels. In addition, each viewpoint has been carefully edited to maximize a reader's understanding of the content. Short but thorough viewpoints capture the essence of an argument. A substantial, thought-provoking essay question placed at the end of each viewpoint asks the student to further investigate the issues raised in the viewpoint, compare and contrast two authors' arguments, or consider how one might go about forming an opinion on the topic at hand. Each viewpoint contains sidebars that include at-a-glance information and handy statistics. A Facts About section located in the back of the book further supplies students with relevant facts and figures.

Following in the tradition of the Opposing Viewpoints series, Greenhaven Press continues to provide readers with invaluable exposure to the controversial issues that shape our world. As John Stuart Mill once wrote: "The only way in which a human being can make some approach to knowing the whole of a subject is by hearing what can be said about it by persons of every variety of opinion and studying all modes in which it can be looked at by every character of mind. No wise man ever acquired his wisdom in any mode but this." It is to this principle that Introducing Issues with Opposing Viewpoints books are dedicated.

Introduction

"America's public enemy number one in the United States is drug abuse. In order to fight and defeat this enemy, it is necessary to wage a new, all-out offensive."

—President Richard Nixon, June 17, 1971

President Nixon's remarks over forty years ago prompted a turning point in drug policy in the United States. His speech in the Briefing Room at the White House followed a meeting with leaders in Congress and thus began America's war on drugs. In 1973 the Drug Enforcement Administration (DEA) was created with a budget of $75 million. Forty years later that budget had increased to over $2 billion.

The Controlled Substances Act (CSA) of 1970 made the manufacture, importation, possession, use, and distribution of certain substances subject to federal regulation. The CSA categorizes drugs according to perceived risk of abuse and accepted medical uses. Certain drugs, such as heroin and marijuana, have been determined by the federal government to have a high risk of abuse without any legitimate medical use and, therefore, to be illicit under all circumstances. Other drugs that are considered as having a risk of abuse or dependence but also as having accepted medical uses are available only by prescription. Drugs in this category include cocaine, methamphetamine, and various prescription drugs.

Federal law regulates the criminal penalties, including fines and imprisonment, that may be imposed for a conviction of a violation of the CSA. Penalties for drug trafficking at the federal level—meaning for trafficking within or across state lines, from outside the United States, or within the District of Columbia—depend on the quantity of drugs involved, and sentences vary from a fine to life imprisonment. Penalties for simple possession at the federal level range from a fine to three years' imprisonment. However, there are mandatory minimum sentences for possessing certain amounts and for repeat offenders. In addition to federal laws, each state has its own laws regulating the criminal penalties for the manufacture, distribution, and possession of illegal drugs.

The social justification often given for the strict regulation of drugs is to protect both the drug user and society from harm. Illegal drugs are categorized as having a high risk of abuse and dependence, thus the potential for harm to the user is great. In addition, these drugs are seen as having a high social cost from the crime, medical costs, and lowered productivity caused by drug use and drug addiction. Whether or not criminalizing this behavior is the best way to manage these potential harms is open to debate.

Arguments for drug legalization rarely propose a complete absence of government regulation. After all, legal drugs such as alcohol and tobacco are regulated according to safety, age of legal use, and place of consumption. Additionally, proponents of drug legalization do not always want all drugs treated the same: A majority of Americans favor the legalization of marijuana, but less than 10 percent support the legalization of cocaine, heroin, or methamphetamine.

One of the nuanced distinctions in the drug legalization debate is between *legalization* and *decriminalization*. Drug decriminalization calls for eliminating criminal penalties for drug use, though not always for drug production. In this way, proponents of drug decriminalization stop short of calling for drugs to be regulated like alcohol, but propose that the current criminalization of drug users end. The idea behind decriminalization is that too many negative effects come from drug criminalization—such as the costs of incarcerating drug users—that could be reduced by a policy of decriminalization. Yet, proponents of prohibition contend that criminalization is an important part of reducing drug use and its associated harms to society.

The debate about drug legalization in the United States seems to have reached a tipping point in recent years: A 2012 poll found that almost two-thirds of Americans believe the war on drugs has failed. In recent years countries such as Argentina, the Czech Republic, and Portugal have adopted varying levels of decriminalization or legalization regarding certain drugs. In the United States, medical marijuana is now legal in over one-third of the states, and two states—Colorado and Washington—as well as many municipalities have adopted relaxed policies toward individual marijuana possession for recreational use. The current debates about American drug policy are explored in *Introducing Issues with Opposing Viewpoints: Drug Legalization*, shedding light on this divisive and ongoing contemporary issue.

Chapter 1

Is the Prohibition on Drugs Working?

Police execute a high-risk search warrant on a suspected drug house. After forty years, the war on drugs continues to generate controversy.

The War on Drugs Has Reduced the Drug Problem

"The drug problem is growing smaller and has fallen in response to known, effective measures."

John P. Walters

In the following viewpoint John P. Walters argues that the war against drugs has caused drug use and drug crime to decline. Walters contends that the harms of legalizing drug use are numerous and that instances of drug legalization around the world confirm this. Walters claims that the proponents of legalization are mistaken to argue that the drug war has filled the prisons or that it has caused the proliferation of organized crime in Central America and Mexico. Walters is chief operating officer and executive vice president of the Hudson Institute and the former director of the White House Office of National Drug Control Policy.

AS YOU READ, CONSIDER THE FOLLOWING QUESTIONS:

1. According to the author, illegal drug use is what percentage lower now than in 1979?
2. Walters claims that how many of the 21 million drug users in America need treatment for addiction?
3. According to the author, what is the single greatest reason that Americans enter drug treatment?

Even smart people make mistakes—sometimes surprisingly large ones. A current example is drug legalization, which way too many smart people consider a good idea. They offer three bad arguments.

The Decline in Drug Use

First, they contend, "the drug war has failed"—despite years of effort we have been unable to reduce the drug problem. Actually, as imperfect as surveys may be, they present overwhelming evidence that the drug problem is growing smaller and has fallen in response to known, effective measures. Americans use illegal drugs at substantially lower rates than when systematic measurement began in 1979—down almost 40 percent. Marijuana use is down by almost half since its peak in the late 1970s, and cocaine use is down by 80 percent since its peak in the mid-1980s. Serious challenges with crack [cocaine], meth[amphetamine], and prescription drug abuse have not changed the broad overall trend: Drug use has *declined* for the last 40 years, as has drug crime.

The decades of decline coincide with tougher laws, popular disapproval of drug use, and powerful demand reduction measures such as drug treatment in the criminal justice system and drug testing. The drop also tracks successful attacks on supply—as in the reduction of cocaine production in Colombia and the successful attack on meth production in the United States. Compared with most areas of public policy, drug control measures are quite effective when properly designed and sustained.

Drug enforcement keeps the price of illegal drugs at hundreds of times the simple cost of producing them. To destroy the criminal market, legalization would have to include a massive price cut, dramatically stimulating use and addiction. Legalization advocates typically ignore the science. Risk varies a bit, but *all* of us and a variety of other living things—monkeys, rats, and mice—can become addicted if exposed to addictive substances in sufficient concentrations, frequently enough, and over a sufficient amount of time. It is beyond question that more people using drugs, more frequently, will result in more addiction.

The Lessons of Drug Legalization

About a third of illegal drug users are thought to be addicted (or close enough to it to need treatment), and the actual number is probably higher. There are now at least 21 million drug users, and at least 7 million need treatment. How much could that rise? Well, there are now almost 60 million cigarette smokers and over 130 million who use alcohol each month. It is irrational to believe that legalization would not increase addiction by millions.

We can learn from experience. Legalization has been tried in various forms, and every nation that has tried it has reversed course sooner or later. America's first cocaine epidemic occurred in the late 19th century, when there were no laws restricting the sale or use of the drug. That epidemic led to some of the first drug laws, and the epidemic subsided. Over a decade ago the Netherlands was the model for legalization. However, the Dutch have reversed course, as have Sweden and Britain (twice). The newest example for legalization advocates is Portugal, but as time passes the evidence there grows of rising crime, blood-borne disease, and drug usage.

The lessons of history are the lessons of the street. Sections of our cities have tolerated or accepted the sale and use of drugs. We can see for ourselves that life is not the same or better in these places, it is much worse. If they can, people move away and stay away. Every instance of legalization confirms that once you increase the number of drug users and the addicted, it is difficult to undo your mistake.

The most recent form of legalization—pretending smoked marijuana is medicine—is following precisely the pattern of past failure. The majority of the states and localities that have tried it are moving to correct their mistake, from California to Michigan. Unfortunately, Washington, D.C., is about to start down this path. It will end badly.

Drug Laws and Prison

The second false argument for legalization is that drug laws have filled our prisons with low-level, non-violent offenders. The prison population has increased substantially over the past 30 years, but the popula-

Former US drug czar John P. Walters (pictured at front) claims that the war on drugs has not filled the prisons or caused a proliferation of organized crime in Mexico and Central America.

tion on probation is much larger and has grown almost as fast. The portion of the prison population associated with drug offenses has been declining, not growing. The number of diversion programs for substance abusers who commit crimes has grown to such an extent that the criminal justice system is now the single largest reason Americans enter drug treatment.

Despite constant misrepresentation of who is in prison and why, the criminal justice system has steadily and effectively focused on violent and repeat offenders. The unfortunate fact is that there are too many people in prison because there are too many criminals. With the rare exceptions that can be expected from human institutions, the criminal justice system is not convicting the innocent.

Drugs and Organized Crime

Most recently, crime and violence in Central America and Mexico have become the third bad reason to legalize drugs. Even some foreign leaders have joined in claiming that violent groups in Latin America would be substantially weakened or eliminated if drugs were legal.

Many factors have driven this misguided argument. First, while President Alvaro Uribe in Colombia and President Felipe Calderón in Mexico demonstrated brave and consequential leadership against crime and terror, such leadership is rare. For both the less competent and the corrupt, the classic response in politics is to blame someone else for your failure.

The real challenge is to establish the rule of law in places that have weak, corrupt, or utterly inadequate institutions of justice. Yes, the cartels and violent gangs gain money from the drug trade, but they engage in the full range of criminal activities—murder for hire, human trafficking, bank robbery, protection rackets, car theft, and kidnapping, among others. They seek to control areas and rule with organized criminal force. This is not a new phenomenon, and legalizing drugs will not stop it. In fact, U.S. drug laws are a powerful means of working with foreign partners to attack violent groups and bring their leaders to justice.

Legalization advocates usually claim that alcohol prohibition caused organized crime in the United States and its repeal ended the threat. This is widely believed and utterly false. Criminal organizations existed before and after prohibition. Violent criminal organizations exist until they are destroyed by institutions of justice, by each other, or by authoritarian measures fueled by popular fear. No honest criminal justice official or family in this hemisphere will be safer tomorrow if drugs are legalized—and the serious among them know it.

The Absurdity of Calls for Legalization

Are the calls for legalization merely superficial—silly background noise in the context of more fundamental problems? Does this talk make any difference? Well, suppose someone you know said, "Crack and heroin and meth are great, and I am going to give them to my brothers and sisters, my children and my grandchildren." If you find that statement absurd, irresponsible, or obscene, then at some level you appreciate that drugs cannot be accepted in civilized society. Those who talk of legalization do not speak about giving drugs to their families, of course; they seem to expect drugs to victimize someone else's family.

Irresponsible talk of legalization weakens public resolve against use and addiction. It attacks the moral clarity that supports responsible behavior and the strength of key institutions. Talk of legalization today has a real cost to our families and families in other places. The best remedy would be some thoughtful reflection on the drug problem and what we say about it.

EVALUATING THE AUTHOR'S ARGUMENTS:

In this viewpoint John P. Walters argues that if proponents of drug legalization are not willing to recommend drug use to their family members, then something is wrong with their call for legalization. Is it reasonable to consistently hold that drugs ought to be legalized but that their use should be discouraged? Why or why not?

The War on Drugs Is Not Working

Leonard Pitts Jr.

"The drug war has failed."

In the following viewpoint Leonard Pitts Jr. argues that the drug war has been a failure. Pitts claims that there has been racial injustice in the way the war on drugs has been carried out, and he notes that drug dealers have come to dominate in Mexico in spite of, or even because of, the drug war. Pitts contends that statistics show that the drug war has resulted in numerous arrests, lots of money spent, and a rise in drug use, but no more addiction than almost a century ago. Pitts is a nationally syndicated columnist and the winner of the 2004 Pulitzer Prize for commentary.

AS YOU READ, CONSIDER THE FOLLOWING QUESTIONS:

1. Which demographic serves the vast majority of the nation's drug-related prison time, according to the author?
2. How many Americans have been arrested in connection with the war on drugs, according to Pitts?
3. What percentage of Americans are drug addicted now, according to the author?

If President [Barack] Obama had a son, he would look like Trayvon Martin [black teenager shot to death by George Zimmerman in Sanford, Florida]. So the president famously said.

Racial Inequality in the War on Drugs

And the president's son would thereby find himself at significantly greater risk of running afoul of the so-called "War on Drugs" than, say, a son of [former US president] George W. Bush. Depending on what state he lived in, a Trayvon Obama might be 57 times more likely than a Trayvon Bush to be imprisoned on drug charges.

US president Richard M. Nixon (pictured) started the war on drugs in 1971, stating that "America's public enemy number one in the United States is drug abuse."

This is not because he would be 57 times more likely to commit a drug crime. To the contrary, white American men commit the vast majority of the nation's drug crimes, but African-American men do the vast majority of the nation's drug time. It is a nakedly racial disparity that should leave the U.S. Department of "Justice" embarrassed to call itself by that name.

So it is difficult to be anything but disappointed at President Obama's recent declaration at a summit in Colombia that "legalization is not the answer" to the international drug problem. The president argued that drug dealers might come to "dominate certain countries if they were allowed to operate legally without any constraint." This dominance, he said, "could be just as corrupting if not more corrupting than the status quo."

One wonders if the president forgot to engage brain before operating mouth.

Dealers might "dominate certain countries?" Has Obama never heard of Mexico, that country on our southern border where drug dealers operate as a virtual shadow government in some areas? Is he unfamiliar with Colombia—his host nation—where, for years, the government battled a drug cartel brutal and brazen enough to attack the Supreme Court and assassinate the attorney general? That scenario Obama warns against actually came to pass a long time ago.

The Failure of the War on Drugs

Similarly, it is a mystery how the manufacture and sale of a legal product could be "just as corrupting if not more corrupting than the status quo." How could that be, given that there would no longer be a need for drug merchants to bribe judges, politicians and police for protection? What reason is there to believe a legal market in drugs would be any more prone to corruption than the legal markets in cigarettes and alcohol? Or, popcorn and chocolate?

The president's reasoning is about as sturdy as a cardboard box in a monsoon. Even he must know—who can still deny?—that the drug war has failed. When it comes to quantifying that failure, several numbers are stark and edifying:

- Forty-one. That's how many years the "War" has raged.
- Forty million-plus. That's how many Americans have been arrested.
- One trillion-plus. That's the cost.
- Two thousand, eight hundred. That's the percentage by which drug use has risen.
- One-point-three. That's the percentage of Americans who were drug addicted in 1914.
- One-point-three. That's the percentage of Americans who are drug addicted now.

The numbers come from Law Enforcement Against Prohibition, a group of cops, judges, DEA [Drug Enforcement Administration] agents and other drug warriors who are demanding an end to the drug war. Their statistics call to mind an old axiom: the definition of crazy is to continue doing the same thing but expecting a different result.

Is the Prohibition on Drugs Working?   **19**

The Alternative to the Drug War

That said, it is not difficult to understand why the president—or anyone—might flinch at the notion of legalizing drugs. It is a big, revolutionary idea, an idea that would change the way things have been done since forever. If someone feels a need to pause before crossing that line, that's understandable.

But let none of us do as the president did—hide behind a specious argument that offers no solution, no way forward and, most critically, no leadership.

Drug legalization is not the answer? OK, Mr. President, fair enough. What is?

EVALUATING THE AUTHOR'S ARGUMENTS:

In this viewpoint Leonard Pitts Jr. claims that the war on drugs has failed and urges President Barack Obama to consider legalization or some alternative. What would be an alternative to the current criminalization of drug distribution and drug use and the proposed legalization of all drugs?

The Trend Toward Drug Decriminalization Has Failed

Michael Gerson

"The de facto decrimi-nalization of drugs in some neighborhoods . . . has encouraged widespread addiction."

In the following viewpoint Michael Gerson argues that the libertarian argument for drug legalization is off the mark and that one need only look at the effects of decriminalization to see why. Gerson claims that no freedom results from drug legalization and that conservatism offers an alternative where government plays an important role in protecting liberty, in part by prohibiting drugs. Gerson is a nationally syndicated columnist whose columns appear twice weekly in the *Washington Post.* He is the author of *Heroic Conservatism: Why Republicans Need to Embrace America's Ideals (and Why They Deserve to Fail If They Don't).*

AS YOU READ, CONSIDER THE FOLLOWING QUESTIONS:
1. In what part of the United States does the author claim that drugs have essentially been decriminalized?
2. Which three philosophers does the author suggest are misused by libertarians in supporting their argument for drug legalization?
3. Gerson argues that the proper role of government in cultivating self-governing individuals is through doing what?

Before last week's [May 5, 2011,] South Carolina Republican debate, Ron Paul supporters complained that their candidate was not getting the first-tier attention his polling and fundraising should bring. It is true that Paul has often been overlooked and dismissed, as one might treat a slightly dotty uncle. But perhaps some first-tier scrutiny is deserved.

The Argument for Drug Legalization

Paul was the only candidate at the debate to make news, calling for the repeal of laws against prostitution, cocaine and heroin. The freedom to use drugs, he argued, is equivalent to the freedom of people to "practice their religion and say their prayers." Liberty must be defended "across the board." "It is amazing that we want freedom to

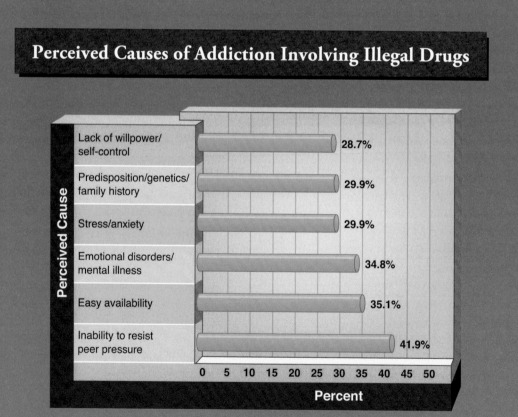

Perceived Causes of Addiction Involving Illegal Drugs

Perceived Cause	Percent
Lack of willpower/self-control	28.7%
Predisposition/genetics/family history	29.9%
Stress/anxiety	29.9%
Emotional disorders/mental illness	34.8%
Easy availability	35.1%
Inability to resist peer pressure	41.9%

Note 1: Respondents could choose two or three answers.
Note 2: Other research finds that genetics account for up to 78% of the risk for the development of addiction involving prescription and other drugs.

Taken from: CASA Columbia *National Addiction Belief and Attitude Survey* (NABAS), 2008. The National Center on Addiction and Substance Abuse at Columbia University (CASA). "Addiction Medicine: Closing the Gap between Science and Practice," June 2012. www.casacolumbia.org.

pick our future in a spiritual way," he said, "but not when it comes to our personal habits."

This argument is strangely framed: If you tolerate Zoroastrianism, you must be able to buy heroin at the quickie mart. But it is an authentic application of libertarianism, which reduces the whole of political philosophy to a single slogan: Do what you will—pray or inject or turn a trick—as long as no one else gets hurt.

Even by this permissive standard, drug legalization fails. The de facto decriminalization of drugs in some neighborhoods— say, in Washington, D.C.—has encouraged widespread addiction. Children, freed from the care of their addicted parents, have the liberty to play in parks decorated by used needles. Addicts are liberated into lives of prostitution and homelessness. Welcome to Paulsville, where people are free to take soul-destroying substances and debase their bodies to support their "personal habits."

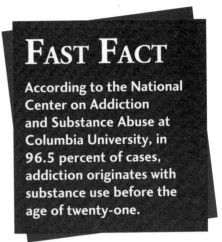

FAST FACT

According to the National Center on Addiction and Substance Abuse at Columbia University, in 96.5 percent of cases, addiction originates with substance use before the age of twenty-one.

The Reality of Libertarianism

But Paul had an answer to this criticism. "How many people here would use heroin if it were legal? I bet nobody would," he said to applause and laughter. Paul was claiming that good people—people like the Republicans in the room—would not abuse their freedom, unlike those others who don't deserve our sympathy.

The problem, of course, is that even people in the room may have sons or daughters who have struggled with addiction. Or maybe even have personal experience with the freedom that comes from alcohol and drug abuse. One imagines they did not laugh or cheer.

Libertarians often cover their views with a powdered wig of 18th- and 19th-century philosophy. They cite [British philosophers John] Locke, [Adam] Smith and [John Stuart] Mill as advocates of a peaceable kingdom—a utopia of cooperation and spontaneous order. But

US congressman and 2012 presidential candidate Ron Paul (pictured) made news at the South Carolina presidential debate when he claimed that the war on drugs had failed. Paul advocated legalizing all drugs.

the reality of libertarianism was on display in South Carolina. Paul concluded his answer by doing a jeering rendition of an addict's voice: "Oh yeah, I need the government to take care of me. I don't want to use heroin, so I need these laws." Paul is not content to condemn a portion of his fellow citizens to self-destruction; he must mock them in their decline. Such are the manners found in Paulsville.

This is not "The Wealth of Nations" or the "Second Treatise of Government." It is Social Darwinism. It is the arrogance of the strong. It is contempt for the vulnerable and suffering.

The Conservative Alternative

The conservative alternative to libertarianism is necessarily more complex. It is the teaching of classical political philosophy and the Jewish and Christian traditions that true liberty must be appropriate to human nature. The freedom to enslave oneself with drugs is the freedom of the fish to live on land or the freedom of birds to inhabit the ocean—which is to say, it is not freedom at all. Responsible, self-governing citizens do not grow wild like blackberries. They are cultivated in institutions—families, religious communities and decent, orderly neighborhoods. And government has a limited but important role in reinforcing social norms and expectations—including laws against drugs and against the exploitation of men and women in the sex trade.

It was just 12 years ago—though it seems like a political lifetime—that a Republican presidential candidate visited a rural drug treatment center outside Des Moines [Iowa]. Moved by the stories of recovering young addicts, Texas Gov. George W. Bush talked of his own struggles with alcohol. "I'm on a walk. And it's a never-ending walk as far as I'm concerned. . . . I want you to know that your life's walk is shared by a lot of other people, even some who wear suits."

In determining who is a "major" candidate for president, let's begin here. Those who support the legalization of heroin while mocking addicts are marginal. It is difficult to be a first-tier candidate while holding second-rate values.

> **EVALUATING THE AUTHOR'S ARGUMENTS:**
>
> In this viewpoint Michael Gerson accuses Ron Paul of mocking addicts by calling for drug legalization. How does Gerson think Paul's call for legalization mocks addicts?

Drug Prohibition, Not Increased Drug Decriminalization, Has Failed

David Boaz

"Drug decriminalization fails? It just ain't so."

In the following viewpoint David Boaz argues that the current prohibition on drugs causes numerous harms and that decriminalization is the answer, not the problem. Boaz claims that the current policy of imprisoning drug users is hypocritical given the fact that the last three presidents have admitted to using illegal drugs. He contends that the prohibition on drugs leads to crime, wasted money, and violence, and he points to a country where he claims decriminalization works. Boaz is the executive vice president of the libertarian think tank the Cato Institute and author of *The Politics of Freedom: Taking on the Left, the Right, and Threats to Our Liberties.*

AS YOU READ, CONSIDER THE FOLLOWING QUESTIONS:
1. According to the author, how many people are arrested each year under current drug laws?
2. Boaz points to an estimate positing that governments could save how much money a year through drug decriminalization?
3. What country does the author give as an example of where the decriminalization of drugs has worked?

Michael Gerson, former speechwriter for President George W. Bush and now a columnist for the *Washington Post,* has denounced libertarianism as "morally empty," "anti-government," "a scandal," "an idealism that strangles mercy," guilty of "selfishness," "rigid ideology," and "rigorous ideological coldness." (He's starting to repeat himself.)

In his May 9 [2011] column, "Ron Paul's Land of Second-Rate Values," he went after Rep. Paul for his endorsement of drug legalization in the Republican presidential debate. "Dotty uncle," he fumed, alleging that Paul has "contempt for the vulnerable and suffering." Paul holds "second-rate values," he added.

FAST FACT

Starting in 2001, Portugal lifted criminal penalties for drug users even though drugs are still illegal and criminal penalties still apply to drug growers, dealers, and traffickers.

What did Paul do to set him off? He said that adult Americans ought to have the freedom to make their own decisions about their personal lives—from how they worship, to what they eat and drink, to what drugs they use. And he mocked the paternalist mindset: "How many people here would use heroin if it were legal? I bet nobody would say, 'Oh yeah, I need the government to take care of me. I don't want to use heroin, so I need these laws.'"

Drug Laws and Jail

Gerson accused Paul of mocking not paternalists but addicts: "Paul is not content to condemn a portion of his fellow citizens to self-destruction;

he must mock them in their decline." Gerson wants to treat them with compassion. But let's be clear: He thinks the compassionate way to treat suffering people is to put them in jail. And in the [2011] California case *Brown v. Plata*, the Supreme Court just reminded us what it means to hold people in prison:

> California's prisons are designed to house a population just under 80,000, but . . . the population was almost double that. The State's prisons had operated at around 200% of design capacity for at least 11 years. Prisoners are crammed into spaces neither designed nor intended to house inmates. As many as 200 prisoners may live in a gymnasium, monitored by as few as two or three correctional officers. As many as 54 prisoners may share a single toilet. Because of a shortage of treatment beds, suicidal inmates may be held for prolonged periods in telephone-booth-sized cages without toilets.

Gerson knows this. His May 27 column quoted this very passage and concluded, "[I]t is absurd and outrageous to treat [prisoners] like animals while hoping they return to us as responsible citizens."

Gerson contrasted the "arrogance" of Paul's libertarian approach to the approach of "a Republican presidential candidate [who] visited a rural drug treatment center outside Des Moines [Iowa]. Moved by the stories of recovering young addicts, Texas Gov. George W. Bush talked of his own struggles with alcohol. 'I'm on a walk. And it's a never-ending walk as far as I'm concerned. . . . I want you to know that your life's walk is shared by a lot of other people, even some who wear suits.'"

Gerson seems to have missed the point of his anecdote. Neither Bush nor the teenagers in a Christian rehab center were sent to jail. They overcame their substance problems through faith and personal responsibility. But Gerson and Bush support the drug laws under which more than 1.5 million people a year are arrested and some 500,000 people are currently in jail.

Our last three presidents have all acknowledged they used illegal drugs in their youth. Yet they don't seem to think—nor does Gerson suggest—that their lives would have been made better by arrest, conviction, and incarceration. If libertarianism is a second-rate value, where does hypocrisy rank?

Estimated Expenditures and Revenues from Drug Legalization, Billions of 2008 Dollars

		Marijuana	Heroin/ Cocaine	Other	All Drugs
Total Expenditures	Local, State, and Federal	8.7	20.0	12.6	41.3
Total Revenues	State and Federal	8.7	32.6	5.5	46.7

Taken from: Jeffrey A. Miron and Katherine Waldock. "The Budgetary Impact of Ending Drug Prohibition." Cato Institute, 2010. www.cato.org.

Decriminalization and Prohibition

Gerson seems to have a fantastical view of our world today. He writes, "[D]rug legalization fails. The de facto decriminalization of drugs in some neighborhoods—say, in Washington, D.C.—has encouraged widespread addiction."

This is mind-boggling. What has failed in Washington, D.C., is drug prohibition. As Mike Riggs of *Reason* magazine wrote, "I want to know where in D.C. one can get away with slinging or using in front of a cop. The 2,874 people arrested by the MPD [D.C. Metropolitan Police Department] for narcotics violations between Jan. 1 and April 9 of this year would probably like to know, too."

Michelle Alexander, author of *The New Jim Crow*, writes, "Crime rates have fluctuated over the past few decades—and currently are at historical lows—but imprisonment rates have soared. Quintupled. And the vast majority of that increase is due to the War on Drugs, a war waged almost exclusively in poor communities of color." Michael Gerson should ask Professor Alexander for a tour of these neighborhoods where he thinks drugs are de facto decriminalized.

In a recent Cato Institute report, Jeffrey Miron of Harvard University estimated that governments could save $41.3 billion a year if they decriminalized drugs, an indication of the resources we're putting into police, prosecutions, and prisons to enforce the war on drugs.

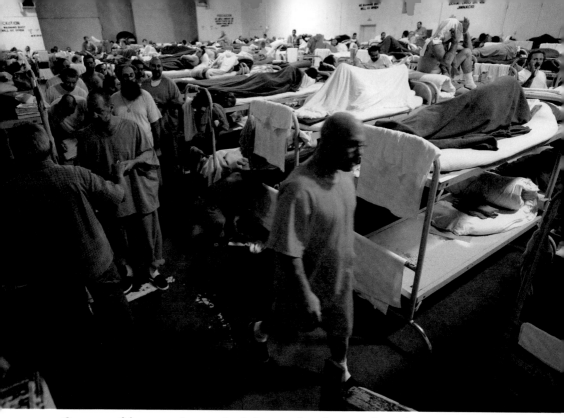

Opponents of the war on drugs say that locking people up for minor drug offensives is hypocritical and causes severe overcrowding in prisons, such as seen here in a California penal facility.

What Gerson correctly observes is communities wracked by crime, corruption, social breakdown, and widespread drug use. But that is a result of the failure of prohibition, not decriminalization. This is an old story. The murder rate rose with the start of alcohol Prohibition, remained high during Prohibition, and then declined for 11 consecutive years when Prohibition ended. And corruption of law enforcement became notorious [during Prohibition].

The Harms of Drug Prohibition

Drug prohibition itself creates high levels of crime. Addicts commit crimes to pay for a habit that would be easily affordable if it were legal. Police sources have estimated that as much as half the property crime in some major cities is committed by drug users. More dramatically, because drugs are illegal, participants in the drug trade cannot go to court to settle disputes, whether between buyer and seller or between rival sellers. When black-market contracts are breached, the result is often some form of violent sanction.

When Gerson writes that "responsible, self-governing citizens . . . are cultivated in institutions—families, religious communities and decent, orderly neighborhoods," he should reflect on what happens to poor communities under prohibition. Drug prohibition has created a criminal subculture in our inner cities. The immense profits to be had from a black-market business make drug dealing the most lucrative endeavor for many people, especially those who care least about getting on the wrong side of the law. Drug dealers become the most visibly successful people in inner-city communities, the ones with money and clothes and cars. Social order is turned upside down when the most successful people in a community are criminals. The drug war makes peace and prosperity virtually impossible in inner cities.

There is a place where drugs have been decriminalized, not just de facto but in law. Maybe Gerson should have cited it instead of Washington, D.C. Trouble is, it doesn't make his point. Ten years ago Portugal decriminalized all drugs. Recently Glenn Greenwald studied the Portuguese experience in a study for the Cato Institute. He reported, "Portugal, whose drug problems were among the worst in Europe, now has the lowest usage rate for marijuana and one of the lowest for cocaine. Drug-related pathologies, including HIV transmission, hepatitis transmission and drug-related deaths, have declined significantly."

Drug decriminalization fails? It just ain't so.

EVALUATING THE AUTHOR'S ARGUMENTS:

In this viewpoint David Boaz argues that drug decriminalization would save governments significant amounts of money. How would Michael Gerson, author of the previous viewpoint, likely respond to this justification?

The War on Drugs Is Destroying Black America

John McWhorter

"The War on Drugs destroys black families."

In the following viewpoint John McWhorter argues that the war on drugs has played a central role in shaping black culture and destroying black families. McWhorter proposes that all drugs be legalized. He claims that an end to the war on drugs will eliminate inner-city violence; cause young black men to get legitimate jobs, thereby rebuilding black families; and improve race relations in America. McWhorter is a senior fellow in public policy at the Manhattan Institute, a contributing editor to the institute's *City Journal*, and author of *Winning the Race: Beyond the Crisis in Black America*.

AS YOU READ, CONSIDER THE FOLLOWING QUESTIONS:

1. According to the author, why does the war on drugs discourage young black men from seeking legal employment?
2. McWhorter proposes that legalizing drugs would entail the second half of the rescue of black America, the first half being what?
3. The author says that what attempts to address the problems in black America over the last forty years have not worked?

The War on Drugs destroys black families. It has become a norm for black children to grow up in single-parent homes, their fathers away in prison for long spells and barely knowing them. In poor and working-class black America, a man and a woman raising their children together is, of all things, an unusual sight. The War on Drugs plays a large part in this. It must stop.

The War on Drugs' Effect on the Black Community

The War on Drugs discourages young black men from seeking legal employment. Because the illegality of drugs keeps the prices high, there are high salaries to be made in selling them. This makes selling drugs a standing tempting alternative to seeking lower-paying legal employment. The result is usually spells in jail, as well as a failure to build the job skills for legal employment that serve as a foundation for a productive existence in middle and later life. The idea that the problem is an absence of job opportunities is refuted by the simple fact that immigrants, including black ones, regularly make do. It is often said that because immigrants have a unique initiative or "pluck" in relocating to the United States in the first place, it is unfair to compare black Americans to them. However, the War on Drugs has made it impossible to see whether black Americans would exhibit such "pluck" themselves if drug selling were not a tempting alternative. High black employment rates in the past gave all indication that black men are no strangers to "pluck" when circumstances require it.

The War on Drugs makes spending time in prison a badge of honor. To black men involved in the drug trade, enduring prison time, regarded as an unjust punishment for merely selling people something they want (with some justification), is seen as a badge of strength: the ex-con is a hero rather than someone who went the wrong way. In the 1920s, before the War on Drugs, black Americans, regardless of class level, did not view black ex-cons as heroes.

The War on Drugs' effects on the black community are impervious to community calls for discipline and leadership. Young black men will not be wooed from selling drugs by black leaders calling for families to take responsibility for their children and keep them off of the streets. There are no national black leaders today who have this kind of influence over a significant portion of black people, and there is simply no chance that the NAACP [National Association for the Advancement of Colored People], committed to antidiscrimination activities rather than community uplift, would preach in a constructive fashion any time soon, if ever—and then, black America is too diverse today for the NAACP or the National Urban League to have any serious effect upon all. The days when the White House could invite a quorum of black people considered "representatives of the race" is over. If this were attempted today, one can imagine assorted celebrities invited: [talk show host] Oprah Winfrey, [movie director] Spike Lee, [minister and civil rights activist] Al Sharpton, [minister and civil rights activist] Jesse Jackson, [children's advocate] Marian Wright Edelman, [politician and civil rights activist] John Lewis, [comedian] Bill Cosby, and so on. But these people do not determine what black America as a whole thinks or does. These people do not have the wherewithal to translate their verdicts into federal policy.

A Proposal to Legalize Drugs

What will turn black America around for good is the elimination of a policy that prevents too many people from doing their best. Legalizing marijuana is just a start, and reducing the length of sentences for possession of crack cocaine would address only the tip of the iceberg. While efforts in this vein are laudable, they would not reduce the basic financial incentive for engaging in the drug trade in the first place, and thus would leave the associated cultural pattern in place. Since the 1980s, as sentences for possessing or selling drugs have become lengthier, the price of cocaine on the street has become cheaper.

Make no mistake—I propose that hard drugs be available for purchase for prices below anything that could make a living for someone selling them on the street. They should be available in maintenance doses, possibly for free. Resources now tied up in useless enforcement would be used for truly effective rehabilitation programs. Fears of an

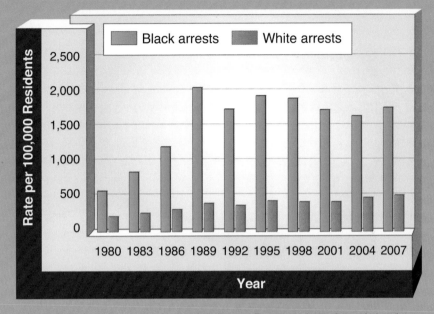

US Rates of Adult Drug Arrests by Race, 1980–2007

Note: Rates of arrest calculated using US Census Bureau estimated population data for each year.

Taken from: Human Rights Watch. "Decades of Disparity: Drug Arrests and Race in the United States," March 2009. www.hrw.org.

addiction epidemic are unfounded: none such has occurred in Portugal, where the drug war has been significantly scaled back. Our discomfort with the idea of heroin available at drug stores is similar to that of a Prohibitionist shuddering at the thought of bourbon available at the corner store. We'll get over it—because we should, and we must.

The elimination of the War on Drugs would entail completing the other half of the rescue of black America that welfare reform contributed in 1996. Open-ended, rather than time-limited, welfare prevented too many black women from doing their best from the late sixties to 1996. The women themselves readily confirm this, and the higher employment rates among them immediately after 1996 prove that this was the case.

The war on drugs has had a disproportionate effect on African Americans. Black men make up over 40 percent of the prison population but are only 14 percent of the US population.

In 1996 countless people genuinely thought black women would wind up shivering on sidewalk grates. These people underestimated the basic human resilience of black people. In the same way, if the War on Drugs is ended, the same kinds of people will assume that young black men will wander about jobless and starving. They will not, because they are human beings with basic resilience and survival instincts.

The Effects of Ending the War on Drugs

Let's imagine a black America with no War on Drugs.

No more gang wars over turf, no more kids shooting each other over sneakers, no more "Stop the Violence" rallies, no more agonized discussions about gun possession in the inner city. Quite simply, people who don't sell drugs for a living don't much need to kill each other over turf.

No more glum speculations about the extent to which black women's romantic choices are shaped by a "shortage of black men," no more scholarship showing that women in the ghetto get pregnant out of wedlock because they don't see the men they know as marriageable. Because there's no War on Drugs, there are no more black men up the river proportionally than white, Latino, or Asian men—because the men get jobs, as they did in the old days, even in the worst ghettos, because they have to. Black communities are now full to bursting with men, black women have their pick of them, and we can move on.

No more does a privileged man like [Harvard professor] Henry Louis Gates shout, "Why, because I'm a black man in America?" when questioned by a policeman.[1] Gates' take on being asked why he was breaking and entering into his own house was understandable in an America with a War on Drugs that forces cops to pay special attention to young black men. With the War on Drugs eliminated, the cops would have no reason to do this, and the understandable paranoia of men like Gates would evaporate.

The Impact on Race Relations

No more calls for a "conversation" about race, with the real intention being that black people get to vent at white people and reveal to them the precious wisdom that racism remains more important than you might think. Because there is no longer a sense that black America is under siege, no one is wasting time dreaming of this impossible "conversation."

The hideous drop-out rate among ghetto teens? Watch it fall as soon as there's no way to keep money in your pocket without a diploma.

---

1. Gates was arrested in July 2009 when police thought he was breaking into a house in Cambridge, Massachusetts, which turned out to be his own home. The incident precipitated a national discussion on racial profiling by police.

The War on Drugs gives ghetto males an ever-standing option for making a living without staying in school.

Do you often get a sense that many black people operate according to a belief that they are not subject to the same rules as everyone else, in terms of civility, achievement, and life plans? You probably do, and frankly, you are seeing something real. There is a kind of black person who does feel that the rules are different for him. And what underlies this, although most would not put it in so many words, is the relationship between black men and the police. Ask a black person why they think racism still defines black lives, if they do, and count how many seconds pass before they start talking about the police. Upon which, return to my point here: with no War on Drugs, a generation would grow up without that prickly, defensive sense of what being black means.

No more exaggeration, double-talk, melodrama, no more formulaic rage, no more staged indignation. Imagine all of the energy wasted on this devoted to real things, like schools, diet, and health care.

The Need to Try Something Else

There will be those who say that I am exaggerating the centrality of the War on Drugs to black America's problems. I believe that they are wrong, and the question we must ask is: What do you suggest?

We hope that they do not suggest more of what's been going on for the past 40 years: sonorous phrasings at forums and meetings and on websites and blogs about responsibility, expectations, institutional racism, and profile articles about individuals making a difference for a few dozen people at a time in a particular city for a few years before life moves them on.

Franklin D. Roosevelt said "Take a method and try it. If it fails, admit it and try another. But above all, try something." What do you suggest we *try* instead? Community centers? Take a look at the track record on that. Or is it that we have to try a lot of things all at the same time? Well, what else have we been doing for 40 years, and where are we now? He who supposes that a random combination of unfocused, usually temporary and largely ineffective things is preferable to trying something else is responsible for explaining why, and he could not.

Let's work on something concrete. End the War on Drugs and make a better America. This is not about Tune In, Turn On, Drop

Out. This is not about political partisanship. This is about making black lives better—and through that, making America better. That is, not "America" in some vague, poetic sense, but the daily lives that all of us lead.

If we truly want to get past race in this country, we must be aware that it will never happen until the futile War on Drugs so familiar to us now is a memory. All it will take is a single generation of black Americans growing up in a post-Prohibition America for us to get where we all want to go. The time to end the War on Drugs, therefore, is yesterday.

EVALUATING THE AUTHOR'S ARGUMENTS:

In this viewpoint John McWhorter claims that young black men are tempted away from legal employment and into selling drugs. How do you think he would explain why this is a particular problem for the black community and not, for instance, the immigrant or white community?

Keep Fighting Drugs

Artur Davis

"The overheated arguments against the War on Drugs are an unwelcome sign that the politics of victimization are hardly dying out."

In the following viewpoint Artur Davis contends that the arguments for eliminating the war on drugs because of its effects on black America are misguided and dangerous. Davis argues that although the drug war has some flaws, these can be addressed by remedies short of decriminalizing or legalizing drugs. Davis denies that the war on drugs is the cause of destructive trends in distressed communities and so denies that ending the war will help. Davis served from 2003 to 2011 in the US House of Representatives representing Alabama's Seventh District as a Democrat and in 2012 switched political parties and became a Republican.

AS YOU READ, CONSIDER THE FOLLOWING QUESTIONS:

1. The author contends that the war on drugs has led to what problems regarding prisons?
2. Davis suggests what five causes of inner-city alienation as alternatives to the argument that such alienation is caused by the war on drugs?
3. Davis claims that the argument that incarceration and punishment drive poverty in the black community is the Left's mimicking of what bias on the Right?

G *iving up is not an answer.*

The drumbeat is starting on the left over what an embold-ened, reenergized Barack Obama should focus on in his sec-ond term. (There is the inconvenience of an election first, but poll-ing numbers and the job-creation data are inviting enough to make Democrats giddy and eager to drop any veil of centrist intentions.) On the African-American left, the momentum is building for a roll-back of the War on Drugs. This is a consistently vague agenda; it shifts from legalizing marijuana, to freeing police resources for more urgent matters, to comprehensive sentencing reform, and all points in between. But at its worst, it is a dangerously misplaced priority, and a sad reminder of the leadership vacuum in the one community that is trapped in a depression.

To be sure, critics of the War on Drugs have some indisputable facts on their side: Prisons at the federal and state level are crowded with relatively inconsequential, low-level dealers who are hardened by their stint behind bars, and who are often rendered permanently voteless and jobless when they resurface. A disproportionate number of those men, and ever so occasionally women, are black, a factor that helps give prisons the ugly look of a barricaded ghetto. (See Michelle Alexander's best-seller *The New Jim Crow*.) Add to that the disparities in how our laws punish dealing in cocaine as opposed to methamphetamine or marijuana—or even "crack," the rock-like substance derived from cocaine powder—and we see that the current system is outlandishly complex as well as unfair. Finally, there is the poor "kill" rate for the kingpins who are the intended targets. The war never keeps pace with the almost instantaneous succession rate in the drug trade; the critics even contend that aggressive prosecution only pumps up the illicit-drug market, by running up the value of drugs as a threatened commodity.

Most of these flaws have a valid remedy that policymakers should consider. (The supply-and-demand theory is the flimsiest; it would apply only in a fantasy world in which all narcotics were legal and unrestricted.) For example, there ought to be wide reforms in the criminal-justice process. Federal judges should have the flexibility to depart from mandatory minimums in crack cases; the innovation of drug courts, introduced in some localities, ought to be explored in the federal system, along with a range of alternative-sentencing options for small-time players. There are appalling weaknesses in the bar of court-appointed lawyers for indigent defendants (especially at the state level), which result in too many felony guilty pleas by first-time offenders. All these shortcomings need to be addressed.

But the War's sharpest critics would probably consider all of the above to be piecemeal and tepid. Their rhetoric, if not their specific proposals, suggests that they would be dissatisfied with any regime that stresses incarceration and punishment, and that they would distrust even a system that treats the bit players differently from the ringleaders. According to this view, the status quo is so steeped in disparity and so invidious in its purpose that it would take something quite close to disarmament to undo the damage.

Michelle Alexander's recent work, for example, explicitly ties the origins of the War to the rise in conservative, law-and-order politics and to a backlash against the assertiveness of the civil-rights movement. Her charge ignores the objective facts that (1) the crack trade exponentially expanded in the Eighties, and (2) the users who were maimed by the drugs and their trade were overwhelmingly African-American. Her book offers a strangely sympathetic treatment of the viciously predatory men who ran that trade and built mini-fortunes from it. Instead of being Alexander's lost generation, they were essentially murderers whose weapons of choice were vials and pipes, and who did their killing from a distance; it is horribly implausible to suggest that without a crackdown on drugs, they were headed for a life of good citizenship. (According to the *New York Times*, James Forman Jr.—son of the civil-rights leader—makes a version of this argument in an upcoming article in the *New York University Law Review*. He makes the equally valid point that drug offenders are less than a fourth of the current prison population.)

John McWhorter, in *The New Republic*, makes a claim even more circuitous than Alexander's: that it's the drug crackdown—and not the drug epidemic itself, or the explosion of births out of wedlock, or crush-

Police arrest a local crack dealer. The author argues that the war on drugs does not victimize the black community.

ing poverty, or abysmal education, or the insidious gang culture—that is responsible for the rise in inner-city alienation. That is a sweeping underestimation of every destructive trend in distressed communities, and it is as single-mindedly wrong as Alexander's effort to read right-wing politics into what was, after all, predominantly a crackdown on black-on-black crime. (It is worth noting that, for all their flaws, drug sentences are the rare instance in which crimes with black victims are consistently punished severely.)

There is of, course, a cruel set of ironies at work here. In associating the devastated lives of young, poor black men so tightly with the War on Drugs, liberals are doing exactly what the most unfeeling conservatives do when they collapse all inner-city black men into vignettes of current and future street criminals. In arguing that incarceration and punishment drive poverty in the black community, the Left is unintentionally mimicking the Right's bias that poverty is secondary to a pattern of criminal irresponsibility in the destruction of the ghetto. In its zeal to encourage a radical scaling back of the drug laws, the Left is short-changing the importance of education, jobs, and community reinvestment—in other words, it is de-emphasizing priorities in the same way the Right is accused of doing.

This is a classic sign of leadership that has analyzed its way into disarray. More pointedly, the overheated arguments against the War on Drugs are an unwelcome sign that the politics of victimization are hardly dying out with the fall of Sharpe James, or the mainstreaming of Al Sharpton, or the exposure of Kwame Kilpatrick. I recall that Jesse Jackson used to talk about new wine being poured into old wineskins.

EVALUATING THE AUTHOR'S ARGUMENTS:

In this viewpoint Artur Davis suggests a focus on education, jobs, and community reinvestment in the black community rather than repealing drug laws. How do you think John McWhorter, author of the previous viewpoint, would respond to this suggestion?

Chapter 2

How Would Drug Legalization Impact Society?

The movement for the legalization of drugs has many supporters and detractors who debate whether drug legalization would be better for society than the current illegality.

Ron Paul and the War on Drugs

Doug Wead

"Decriminal-izing drugs would pump more than $76 billion into the American economy."

In the following viewpoint Doug Wead argues that the war on drugs has failed and that there is evidence that decriminalization of drugs is a better solution. Wead claims that laws criminalizing the manufacturing, distribution, and use of substances create a criminal underclass and an unacceptable incarceration rate. Wead suggests that ending the war on drugs through decriminalization would eliminate these problems. Wead is a historian, author, and former special assistant to former president George H.W. Bush.

AS YOU READ, CONSIDER THE FOLLOWING QUESTIONS:

1. The author claims that which presidential candidate supported decriminalization?
2. How many Americans are arrested each year for drug use, according to Wead?
3. The author claims that in most states it will cost approximately how much to imprison a three-time felon for life?

L ast month the United Nations issued a report admitting that the worldwide war on drugs has failed. Richard Nixon was the first president to use such terminology back in 1971, and subsequent presidents have been hard at it—all with mixed results.

When I served in the Bush, senior White House, it was the common belief that what was needed was an even bigger hammer for the drug problem. A good combination of focused military power and CIA ingenuity would do the trick. We even invaded Panama. But today, the crisis is worse than ever before with no end in sight. Mexico is only a collateral casualty. That country has been ruined by addiction.

Albert Einstein once quipped that "insanity was doing the same thing over and over again, expecting a different result." Barack Obama and all of the new serious GOP presidential candidates offer only more of the same, proving that our drug policy is indeed insane. That is, all presidential candidates except for one. The one exception is Ron Paul, who would decriminalize drugs.

President George W. Bush holds a report that outlines his 2002 battle plan for the war on drugs. Every president since Nixon has implemented such a plan, with varying degrees of success.

This was one of the big reasons I was late to sign up for the Ron Paul revolution. I liked what he said about a return to constitutional government, about stopping the endless wars, about balancing the budget, about reining in America's Empire and paying its bills at home. But what was with this idea of decriminalizing drugs? Wouldn't that make it worse?

Actually, studies have shown that it is exactly how we will one day solve the problem. And that's why even leaders on the religious right, like Pat Robertson, are touting it as a solution.

Imagine us trying to end the use of tobacco in this country by declaring war. Imagine arresting young people selling cigarettes on the street corners. Imagine policemen going into hospitals and arresting people dying of lung cancer and throwing them in jail. Imagine defoliating the tobacco fields of Virginia and North Carolina. Just how far would we have gotten?

Instead, we educated the nation and now the smoke has cleared.

Laws do not solve such problems. Prohibition of alcohol didn't work either. It created a criminal underclass that corrupted the American judicial system and ran some of our largest cities. Drugs are doing the same thing. Last month we discovered that a single border guard had been paid $5 million to let the drugs pass her station. According to a study by a Harvard economist decriminalizing drugs would pump more than $76 billion into the American economy.

Our country has the second highest incarceration rate in the world. Close to 1.5 million Americans are arrested each year for drug use. In the last twenty years almost half of all arrests in America were for marijuana possession or marijuana use. In most states, a three time felon will spend his whole life in prison at a cost of millions of dollars to taxpayers. We are warehousing people on a massive scale. To give you a sense of perspective, in the Soviet Union in 1934, just before the Great Terror and the massive killing began

Taken from: John Schmitt, Kris Warner, and Sarika Gupta. "The High Budgetary Cost of Incarceration." Center for Economic and Policy Research (CEPR), June 2010. www.cepr.net.

in Stalin's famous Gulag camps, he had gathered close to one million prisoners. This is less than the population of our own prison system in America today.

Now, I am not for decriminalizing drugs because I want to use them. I have never tried marijuana or any other illegal substance, which is interesting when you consider that my name is Wead. But I know that our nation's war on drugs hasn't worked. And there is no use pretending otherwise.

I appreciate the good intentions of those who fought this war and their sacrifices and service and their wonderful ideas. For a time, it may have held back the tide and saved lives. But the stakes are higher than ever. Even more lives now hang in the balance.

I supported Ron Paul because of his prescient understanding of the American economy.

His warnings, which seemed farfetched when I first heard them, started happening right before my eyes. Now, I understand that what he has been saying about the war on drugs is equally true.

We are in trouble. It is time to do this right and quit playing politics with such a serious issue. It is time to do the things we need to do and get this done before another generation burns out.

EVALUATING THE AUTHOR'S ARGUMENTS:

In this viewpoint Doug Wead links the nation's incarceration rate to the war on drugs. What does Marie Gottschalk, author of the following viewpoint, say about that link?

The Benefits of Drug Decriminalization or Legalization Are Overstated

Marie Gottschalk

"The projected fiscal benefits of legalization or decriminalization . . . have been vastly overstated."

In the following viewpoint Marie Gottschalk refers to a 2011 book critiquing calls for drug legalization, agreeing that the benefits of decriminalizing or legalizing drugs are often exaggerated. Gottschalk contends that the reality of legalization or decriminalization would be increased consumption of and dependence upon drugs, with costs to society. Furthermore, she says that the alleged economic benefits of legalization or decriminalization are unlikely to be significant. Gottschalk is a professor of political science at the University of Pennsylvania and the author of *The Prison and the Gallows: The Politics of Mass Incarceration in America.*

AS YOU READ, CONSIDER THE FOLLOWING QUESTIONS:
  1. What was the leading cause of accidental death in 2011, according to the author?
  2. If legalization or decriminalization occurred, what does Gottschalk predict would become of the proposed government regulation of drugs and proposed high taxes?
  3. According to Gottschalk, what would happen to the country's incarceration rate if drugs were legalized or decriminalized?

S ince [US president] Richard Nixon launched the war on drugs five decades ago, it has ground on in the face of a mounting pile of evidence that many drug policies cause more harm than good at home and abroad. In [their] deceptively simple book [*Drugs and Drug Policy: What Everyone Needs to Know*], Mark A.R. Kleiman, Jonathan P. Caulkins, and Angela Hawken eviscerate many of the arguments behind the policies that have been the leading weapons in the war on drugs. But they also cast a skeptical eye on some shibboleths [slogans] of the burgeoning drug reform movement. Sometimes snarky but seldom condescending, the authors' penetrating and nuanced critique of the growing calls for legalization is one of the highlights of the book.

Calls for Drug Legalization or Decriminalization

The calls for legalization or decriminalization might sound good on a bumper sticker or a T-shirt, but they obfuscate a messier political and policy reality. Ending the war on drugs is not simply a matter of bringing the troops home. It will entail some unsettling policy and political tradeoffs. We will have to accept certain policies and law enforcement strategies that foster considerably less harm, but at the cost of giving a wink and a nod to certain illegal behavior. Fans of the [television series] *The Wire* who recall police commander Bunny Colvin's aborted experiment with "Hamsterdam" [where police looked the other way instead of enforcing drug laws] will recognize the dilemma.

Despite tens of billions of dollars spent on interdicting drugs from abroad, the supply of drugs has remained steady. The plummeting street price of many illegal drugs over the last few decades is compelling evidence that interdiction has not done much to stem supply. Drug overdoses have increased almost six-fold in the last thirty years. They are now the leading cause of accidental death in the United States, having surpassed motor vehicle accidents for the first time in 2011.

The authors (Kleiman is a professor of public policy at UCLA [University of California, Los Angeles]. Caulkins and Hawken teach at Carnegie Mellon and Pepperdine universities, respectively) contend that advocates of decriminalization and legalization have drawn the wrong lessons from the experiment with Prohibition in the 1920s and '30s. For all the talk of legalization, the fact is that no country in the world

Portugal's former prime minister, José Sócrates (pictured), advocated the decriminalization of drugs in his country as a way to reduce some of the negative social effects of the war on drugs.

Drug Use in Portugal Before and After Decriminalization in 2001

Type of Drug	Prevalence over Lifetime	
	2001	2007
Cannabis	7.6	11.7
Heroin	0.7	1.1
Cocaine	0.9	1.9
Amphetamines	0.5	0.9
Ecstasy	0.7	1.3
LSD	0.4	0.6
Hallucinogenic Mushrooms	–	0.8

Taken from: Institute on Drugs and Drug Addiction. "2010 Report (2009 data) to the EMCDDA (European Monitoring Centre for Drugs and Drug Addiction, 2011. www.emcdda.europa.eu.

"has free legal commerce in cannabis, cocaine, heroin, or methamphetamine." Even a drug reform maverick like Portugal has not come close to legalizing drugs. Portugal regulates drugs today much like how alcohol was regulated during Prohibition in the United States. Since 2001, possession of any drugs for personal use has not been a crime in Portugal but selling drugs can still land you in prison.

Portugal's experiment with across-the-board decriminalization and Holland's more limited experience with decriminalizing cannabis—sort of—through sales for personal use at its "coffee houses" have much to recommend them. But one has to be clear-eyed that decriminalization rests on accepting an uncomfortable legal inconsistency. "As the Dutch say, the front door of the coffee shops—where the customers enter—is (almost) legal, but the back door—where the product comes in—is entirely illegal," Kleiman, Caulkins, and Hawken note. As a consequence, coffee-shop cannabis costs about what illicit cannabis costs elsewhere in Europe and the United States and is not aggressively marketed. This has probably helped to contain cannabis consumption and abuse.

The Reality of Increased Drug Use

If the United States were to widely legalize or decriminalize drugs, consumption of and dependence on drugs would likely increase—at least for a time—while the price and social stigma would decrease. Advocates of legalization argue that tight regulation of drugs through government monopolies, perhaps modeled after the state liquor stores, and high taxes on drugs would offset some of this increase.

That was the hope when the manufacture and sale of alcohol became legal with the end of Prohibition. But the alcohol example is a sobering one. Taxes on alcohol have plummeted in the decades since Prohibition ended in the 1930s and now are much lower than in most European countries. State liquor stores lost out to private ones as a powerful and well-connected liquor industry asserted itself. Well-heeled advertising campaigns helped make alcohol the country's most popular drug and its most widely abused one.

The authors dismiss claims that shifting resources from law enforcement to prevention programs would stem the expected increase in drug consumption and abuse that would come with legalization or decriminalization. Prevention sounds nice in theory, but the reality is that even the top school-based prevention programs have only a limited impact on substance abuse. These programs are not able to tackle the proven risk factors for substance abuse—a single-parent family, a parent or sibling who is a substance abuser, and socializing with peers who use drugs.

> **FAST FACT**
>
> In 2012 the Netherlands began implementation of a new law that bans non-residents from Dutch coffee shops that sell marijuana, based on concerns about a rise in criminality of the Dutch drug trade.

The Overstated Benefits of Legalization and Decriminalization

As for the projected fiscal benefits of legalization or decriminalization, they have been vastly overstated. The war on drugs has not been the primary engine of the country's unprecedented prison growth. Ending the war on drugs will not significantly reduce the country's extraordinary incarceration rate, which is the highest in the world. Legalizing marijuana could provide a tax windfall for some cash-strapped states, but perhaps at the cost of empowering a powerful commercial marijuana industry bent on increasing consumption through Madison Avenue–style marketing campaigns. One alternative is to permit users to grow their own marijuana and to form small consumer-oriented co-ops. But that likely means sacrificing those projected billions in marijuana tax revenues.

Kleiman, Caulkins, and Hawken challenge the conventional wisdom on other fronts. In their view, drug courts are no panacea for the drug problem, despite all the recent hype about them. As for treatment, most people with a substance abuse problem recover fairly rapidly—actually over a period of months or years, not decades—and without intensive professional intervention. Small doses of warning and encouragement from relatives, friends, and family doctors can go a long way toward helping to bring a drug or alcohol habit under control.

EVALUATING THE AUTHOR'S ARGUMENTS:

In this viewpoint Marie Gottschalk claims that the benefits of legalization and decriminalization have been overstated. Ultimately, then, does she oppose such measures? Give evidence from the text to back your answer.

Viewpoint

3

Drug Legalization Would Help Solve the Problem of Mexico's Cartels

"Ending drug prohibition . . . is the only realistic and viable way to put a permanent stop to . . . Mexico's drug traffickers."

Paul Armentano

In the following viewpoint Paul Armentano argues that because American demand for marijuana funds Mexico's drug cartels, legalizing it would weaken the violent cartels' wealth and power. Armentano claims that continuing the old strategy of fighting the supply of marijuana from Mexico increases costs and violence without diminishing the trade, and he proposes the alternative strategy of legalization. Armentano is the deputy director of NORML (National Organization for the Reform of Marijuana Laws) and coauthor of *Marijuana Is Safer: So Why Are We Driving People to Drink?*

Paul Armentano, "How to End Mexico's Deadly Drug War," *The Freeman,* vol. 59, no 10, December 2009.

AS YOU READ, CONSIDER THE FOLLOWING QUESTIONS:
1. Armentano claims that the US drug czar's office reports that what percentage of profits made by Mexican drug cartels come from the exportation and sale of marijuana to the United States?
2. According to Armentano, domestic marijuana arrests have increased annually by how much since 1991?
3. According to the author, what percentage of Americans now favor the legalization of marijuana?

Albert Einstein [the German-born physicist] declared, "The definition of insanity is doing the same thing over and over again and expecting different results." He wasn't describing the federal government's nearly century-long war on drugs but he might as well have been.

Despite ample lip-service for "hope" and "change," the [Barack] Obama administration's cynical response to the escalating drug prohibition–related violence around the Mexican border epitomizes Einstein's oft-quoted observation.

American Money and Mexico's Drug Cartels

Since 2008 more than 7,000 people—over 1,000 last January [2009] alone, including Mexican civilians, journalists, police, and public officials—have been killed in clashes with warring drug traffickers. Wire-service reports estimate that Mexico's drug lords employ over 100,000 soldiers—approximately as many as the Mexican army—and that the cartels' wealth, intimidation, and influence extend to the highest echelons of law enforcement and government. Where do the cartels get their unprecedented wealth and power? By trafficking in illicit drugs—primarily marijuana—over the border into the United States.

The U.S. Office of Drug Control Policy (more commonly known as the drug czar's office) says more than 60 percent of the profits reaped by Mexican drug lords are derived from the exportation and sale of cannabis to the American market. To anyone who has studied the marijuana issue, this figure should come as no surprise. An estimated 100 million Americans age 12 or older—or about 43 percent of the country—admit to having tried pot, a higher percentage, according to the World Health Organization, than any other country on the planet. Twenty-five million Americans admit (on government surveys, no less) to smoking marijuana during the past year, and 15 million say that they indulge regularly. This high demand, combined with the drug's artificially inflated black-market value (pot possession has been illegal under federal law since 1937), now makes cannabis America's top cash crop.

In fact, according to a 2007 analysis by George Mason University professor Jon Gettman, the annual retail value of the U.S. marijuana market is some $113 billion.

How much of this goes directly to Mexican cartels is difficult to quantify, but no doubt the percentage is significant. Government officials estimate that approximately half the marijuana consumed in the United States originates from outside its borders, and they have identified Mexico as far and away America's largest pot provider. Because Mexican-grown marijuana tends to fetch lower prices on the black market than domestically grown weed (a result attributed largely to lower production costs—the Mexican variety tends to be grown outdoors, while an increasing percentage of American-grown pot is produced hydroponically indoors), it remains consistently popular among U.S. consumers, particularly in a down economy. As a result, U.S. law officials now report that some Mexican cartels are moving to the United States to set up shop permanently. A Congressional Research Service report says low-level cartel members are now establishing clandestine growing operations inside the United States (thus eliminating the need to cross the border), as well as partnering with domestic gangs and other criminal enterprises. A March 23 [2009] *New York Times* story speculated that Mexican drug gangs or their affiliates are now active in some 230 U.S. cities, extending from Tucson, Arizona, to Anchorage, Alaska.

In short, America's multibillion-dollar demand for pot is fueling the Mexican drug trade and much of the turf battles and carnage associated with it.

Problems with the U.S. Government's Strategy

So what are the administration's plans to quell the cartels' growing influence and surging violence? Troublingly, the White House appears intent on recycling the very strategies that gave rise to Mexico's infamous drug lords in the first place.

In March [2009] the administration requested $700 million from Congress to "bolster existing efforts by Washington and Mexican President Felipe Calderón's administration to fight violent trafficking in drugs . . . into the United States." These efforts, as described by the *Los Angeles Times*, include: "vowing to send U.S. money, manpower, and technology to the southwestern border" and "reducing illegal flows (of drugs) in both directions across the border." The administration also announced that it intends to clamp down on the U.S. demand for illicit drugs by increasing funding for drug treatment and drug courts.

There are three primary problems with this strategy.

First, marijuana production is a lucrative business that attracts criminal entrepreneurs precisely because it is a black-market (and highly sought after) commodity. As long as pot remains federally prohibited its retail price to the consumer will remain artificially high, and its production and distribution will attract criminal enterprises willing to turn to violence (rather than the judicial system) to maintain their slice of the multi-billion-dollar pie.

Second, the United States is already spending more money on illicit-drug law enforcement, drug treatment, and drug courts than at any time in our history. FBI data show that domestic marijuana arrests have increased from under 300,000 annually in 1991 to over 800,000 today. Police seizures of marijuana have also risen dramatically in recent years, as has the amount of taxpayer dollars federal officials have spent on so-called "educational efforts" to discourage the drug's use. (For example, since the late 1990s Congress has appropriated well over a billion dollars in anti-pot public service announcements alone.) Yet despite these combined efforts to discourage demand, Americans use more pot than anyone else in the world.

Third, law enforcement's recent attempts to crack down on the cartels' marijuana distribution rings, particularly new efforts launched by the Calderón administration in Mexico, are driving the unprecedented

Demonstrators march in Mexico City on May 5, 2012, for the decriminalization of marijuana. Many see this as a way to reduce violence by drug cartels.

wave in Mexican violence—not abating it. The *New York Times* states: "A crackdown begun more than two years ago by President Felipe Calderón, coupled with feuds over turf and control of the organizations, has set off an unprecedented wave of killings in Mexico. . . . Many of the victims were tortured. Beheadings have become common." Because of this escalating violence, Mexico now ranks behind only Pakistan and Iran as the administration's top international security concern.

An Alternative Strategy

Despite the rising death toll, drug war hawks at the U.S. Drug Enforcement Administration (DEA) remain adamant that the United States' and Mexico's "supply side" strategies are in fact successful. "Our view is that the violence we have been seeing is a signpost of the success our very courageous Mexican counterparts are having," acting DEA administrator Michele Lionhart said recently. "The cartels are acting out like caged animals, because they are caged animals." President Obama also appears to share this view. After visiting with the Calderón government in April, he told CNN he intended to "beef up" security on the border. When asked whether the administration would consider alternative strategies, such as potentially liberalizing pot's criminal classification, Homeland Security Secretary Janet Napolitano replied that such an option "is not on the table."

By contrast the Calderón administration appears open to the idea of legalizing marijuana—or at least reducing criminal sanctions on the possession of small quantities of drugs—as a way to stem the tide of violence. Last spring Mexican lawmakers made the possession of personal-use quantities of cannabis and other illicit substances a non-criminal offense. And in April Mexico's ambassador to the United States, Arturo Sarukhan, told CBS's *Face the Nation* that legalizing the marijuana trade was a legitimate option for both the Mexican and U.S. governments. "[T]hose who would suggest that some of these [legalization] measures be looked at understand the dynamics of the drug trade," Sarukhan said.

Former Mexican President Vicente Fox recently echoed Sarukhan's remarks, as did a commission of former Latin American presidents. "I believe it's time to open the debate over legalizing drugs," Fox told CNN in May. "It can't be that the only way [to try to control illicit drug use] is for the state to use force."

Writing recently on CNN.com, Harvard economist and *Freeman* contributor Jeffrey Miron said that ending drug prohibition—on both sides of the border—is the only realistic and viable way to put a permanent stop to the rising power and violence associated with Mexico's drug traffickers. "Prohibition creates violence because it drives the drug market underground," he wrote. "This means buyers and sellers cannot resolve their disputes with lawsuits, arbitration or advertising, so they resort to violence instead. . . . The only way to reduce violence, therefore, is to legalize drugs."

Growing Support for Marijuana Legalization

Americans' support for legalizing the regulated production and sale of cannabis—an option that would not likely rid the world of cartels, but would arguably reduce their primary source of income—is at an all-time high. In May [2009] a national Zogby telephone poll of 3,937 voters by the Republican-leaning O'Leary Report discovered, for the first time ever, that a slight majority (52 percent) of Americans "favor the legalization of marijuana." A separate Zogby poll reported even stronger support (58 percent) among west-coast voters.

Predictably, critics of marijuana legalization claim that such a strategy would do little to undermine drug traffickers' profit margins because cartels would simply supplement their revenues by selling greater quantities of other illicit drugs. Although this scenario sounds plausible in theory, it appears to be far less likely in practice.

As noted, Mexican drug lords derive an estimated 60 to 70 percent of their illicit income from pot sales. (By comparison, only about 28 percent of their profits are derived from the distribution of cocaine, and less than 1 percent comes from trafficking methamphetamine.) It is unrealistic to think that cartels could feasibly replace this void by stepping up their sales of cocaine, methamphetamine or heroine—all of which remain far less popular among U.S. drug consumers anyway. Just how much less? U.S. Department of Health and Human Services survey data show that roughly two million Americans use cocaine, compared to 15 million for pot. Fewer than 600,000 use methamphetamine, and fewer than 155,000 use heroin. In short, this is hardly the sort of demand that would keep Mexico's drug barons in the lucrative lifestyle to which they've become accustomed.

Of course, it's unrealistic to think that pot legalization would wipe out prohibition-inspired violence altogether. After all, ending alcohol prohibition in America didn't single-handedly put the Mafia out of business (though it greatly reduced its power and influence). And it's always possible that Mexico's drug cartels would continue to engage in violent acts toward one another as competing factions fought over the crumbs of America's drastically shrunken illicit-drug market.

That said, it's equally unrealistic, if not more so, to think that continuing our same failed drug war policies will do anything but exponentially increase the catastrophe they've spawned, both in Mexico and at home. It's time to engage in a different strategy. It's time to seriously consider legalizing marijuana and other drugs.

EVALUATING THE AUTHOR'S ARGUMENTS:

In this viewpoint Paul Armentano argues that depriving Mexican cartels of money by legalizing marijuana in the United States is good policy. Based on what he says here, can a strong argument also be made for legalizing cocaine? Why or why not?

Legalizing Drugs Won't Stop Mexico's Brutal Cartels

"'[Drug] legalization is a fake solution to the problem of [Mexican] security.'"

Elizabeth Dickinson

In the following viewpoint Elizabeth Dickinson argues that there is little reason to think that drug legalization would weaken the cartels that operate in Mexico and elsewhere in Latin America. Dickinson claims that the cartels have expanded far beyond drug trafficking, so that shrinking the drug trade will not have the destructive effect that many proponents of legalization hope. Dickinson concludes that the solution to the cartels lies elsewhere. Dickinson is Persian Gulf correspondent for the *National* newspaper, covering the countries of the Arabian Peninsula from her base in Abu Dhabi, United Arab Emirates.

AS YOU READ, CONSIDER THE FOLLOWING QUESTIONS:

1. According to the author, from 2006 to 2010 annual deaths attributed to drug violence rose by how much?
2. Dickinson claims that in 2008 the cartels employed how many people in the drug trade?
3. According to Dickinson, what four crimes have risen dramatically since 2006?

L *ike all good multinational businesses, they've diversified.*

Mexico City—When the U.N. Office on Drugs and Crime (UNODC) releases its annual status report on the narcotics trade later this month, it will almost certainly show a decrease in the volume of cocaine traveling through Mexico into the United States. Last year's report did too—a 40 percent drop in seizures between 2006 and 2008. Worldwide, the cocaine market today is worth about half as much as it was just 15 years ago—$88 billion compared with $165 billion in 1995.

This would be excellent news—if it weren't for some alarming trends going in the other direction. As the cocaine trade through Mexico has fallen dramatically, the violence here has risen remarkably. Whereas 2006 saw just over 2,000 deaths attributed to drug violence, in 2010 there were an estimated 11,000 such killings, according to data from Stratfor and local press accounts. Ciudad Juárez, a border city of approximately 2 million at the center of the ongoing violence, has seen a particularly sharp spike. In 2001, there were just 16 murders for every 100,000 Ciudad Juárez residents. In 2010, that number reached 93—an increase of nearly sixfold—according to the Mexican Commission for the Defense and Promotion of Human Rights.

In other words, the war on drugs may be taking its toll on the narcotics trade, but it hasn't done anything to end the violence—a stubborn fact that runs counter to an emerging consensus about the drug war. Across Latin America, intellectuals, scholars, and even policymakers are increasingly arguing that there is just one thing that can bring an end to the narco-troubles: the decriminalization of the drug trade in the United States. Legalize and regulate use, proponents argue, and prices would drop and the illicit trade would disappear overnight. Cartels would be starved of their piece of the global illicit drug pie, which the UNODC has estimated at some $320 billion per year.

But would legalization really work? With each day that passes, it looks like it wouldn't be enough, for one overarching reason: The cartels are becoming less like traffickers and more like mafias. Their currency is no longer just cocaine, methamphetamines, or heroin, though they earn revenue from each of these products. As they have grown in size and ambition, like so many big multinational corporations, they have diversified. The cartels are now active in all types of illicit markets, not just drugs.

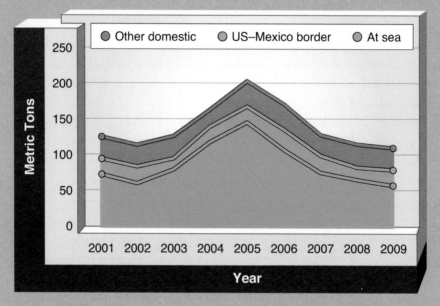

Cocaine Seizures in the United States by Location and Quantity, 2001–2009

- Other domestic
- US–Mexico border
- At sea

Metric Tons

250
200
150
100
50
0

2001 2002 2003 2004 2005 2006 2007 2008 2009

Year

Taken from: United Nations Office on Drugs and Crime (UNODC). "World Drug Report," 2011. www.unodc.org.

"Mexico is experiencing a change with the emergence of criminal organizations that, rather than being product-oriented—drug trafficking—are territorial based," says Antonio Mazzitelli, head of the UNODC office in Mexico City. They now specialize in running protection rackets of all kinds, he says, which might explain why the violence has gotten so bad: Mafias enforce their territorial control by force, killing anyone who resists or gets in the way.

"Before, we had organized crime, but operating strictly in narcotrafficking," adds Eduardo Guerrero Gutiérrez, a consultant and former advisor to the Mexican presidency. "Now we have a type of mafia violence . . . and they are extorting from the people at levels that are incredibly high—from the rich, from businesses." For this reason, Mazzitelli says, legalization would have "little effect."

Cartels such as the Zetas and La Familia, long categorized as drug-trafficking organizations, have transformed themselves into territorial overlords. With distinctive zones of influence, complex organizations, and a wealth of manpower on which to draw, they act as shadow governments in the areas they control, collecting "taxes" on local establishments and taking a cut of the profits from illegal immigration to the United States. "This fight is not solely or primarily to stop drug trafficking," Mexican President Felipe Calderón told the U.S. Congress in May 2010. "The aim is to ensure the safety of Mexican families, who are under threat of abuse and wanton acts of criminals."

The cartels' expansion may have begun through their everyday narcotrafficking work—namely through money laundering, one of the most discussed topics in Mexican politics today. Once upon a time, this was quite easy to do; cartels could wire the money in convoluted ways or open new accounts to which individuals would report earnings from businesses that existed only on paper.

But as the government cracked down in recent years, the cartels got more creative. In June 2010, Mexican authorities put strict limits on how much cash any individual could deposit into a bank on any given day or in any given month. They also limited the amount of cash one could use to buy things like airplanes or cars. So the cartels started engaging in actual trade, which helps them launder their drug profits, explains Shannon O'Neil, a fellow at the Council on Foreign Relations in Washington. They buy consumer goods, such as televisions and perfumes, in the United States and sell them on the Mexican side at a loss. The revenues are "clean" money. And as a bonus, the cartels have a network of vendors ready and willing to sell illicit goods.

Other markets are entirely separate from the narcotics business. Perhaps the most dramatic example is oil, one of Mexico's largest exports and increasingly a vehicle for illicit trade. On June 1, the country's national oil company, Pemex, filed a lawsuit accusing nine U.S. companies of colluding with criminals linked to the drug trade to sell an estimated $300 million worth of stolen oil since 2006. That's an amount equal to the entire cocaine market in Mexico, says UNODC's Mazzitelli. In other words, if the cocaine trade dried up, the cartels would still have access to an equally large source of revenue.

Equally troubling is the firearms trade, which has a direct link both to the violence and to the sustainment of the criminal organizations working across this country of 107 million. There are no reliable estimates of just how big this market is, but according to a recent U.S.

Senate investigation, some 87 percent of the weapons used by the cartels are sourced from the United States. "If this were Southeast Asia, they'd be bombing the gun stores in Arizona, as if that's the Ho Chi Minh trail," says Ted Lewis, head of the human rights program at Global Exchange.

Mexico's cartels have also infiltrated the government and security forces, though primarily at a local level. "Just going by all the reports—academic and media—we could safely assume that all municipal police departments are infiltrated," argues Walter McKay, a security consultant who has spent the last three years working in Mexico. "But it's not just the police. We focus on police and police corruption, but the entire apple is rotten." In the latest example of how high the rot goes, the ex-mayor of Tijuana, Jorge Hank Rhon, was recently arrested for gunrunning and alleged links to organized crime.

Then there is the cartels' sheer size. An estimated 468,000 people worked in the drug trade in 2008, making the cartels collectively among the biggest industries in Mexico. (By comparison, the state oil company, the largest firm in Mexico, has about 360,000 employees.) The cartels also now outnumber the police, estimated at just over 400,000 personnel nationwide in 2010.

The corruption and weakness of the police explains why, over the last half-decade, Calderón has deployed 50,000 troops across the country to decapitate the cartels' leadership and reclaim their territory block by block. Take away a criminal organization's leadership and turf, the thinking goes, and you also rob it of the ability to control just about every market—not just the narcotics trade. Just on Tuesday, June 21, the government apprehended José de Jesús "El Chango" Méndez, leader of the so-called "Knights Templar" cartel. Calderón quickly touted the arrest as a "coup by the federal police against organized crime" on Twitter.

Soldiers and forensic personnel surround the corpses of slain members of the drug cartel La Familia. Deaths in Mexico from cartel violence rose from two thousand in 2006 to eleven thousand in 2010.

Yet critics of the government's strategy say it has been far too militarized. Violence has increased every year since the drug war began, and many civil society groups here accuse the national security forces of hurting as many civilians as they do actual criminals. And even "success" risks a "balloon effect," as a cartel squeezed in one location will almost inevitably pop up elsewhere. This effect is already painfully visible in Latin America as a whole, with Mexican cartels such as the Zetas moving into Guatemala and overwhelming the much-weaker state.

Many activists are thus calling for a completely new approach. Silvano Cantú, a researcher at the Mexican Commission for the Defense and Promotion of Human Rights, argues that Mexico needs to think bigger than trying to win back its turf city by city. "We need to be talking to everyone," he says, mentioning the United States, Colombia, Europe, and "anywhere they clean money and buy arms." The government, too, is frustrated with the guns; cutting down on the sale in the United States is one of the Calderón administration's key demands.

The legalizers, a group that includes former heads of state from Brazil, Colombia, and Mexico, largely agree with this comprehensive approach. Trying to cut supply without cutting demand is a losing game, they argue. "The global war on drugs has failed, with devastating consequences for individuals and societies around the world," they wrote in the most recent report of the Global Commission on Drug Policy, an independent panel that has called for a dramatic rethinking of the drug war. Their recommendations call for the normalization of drugs (that is, legalization of possession linked with public-health regulation), including cocaine.

That would almost certainly hurt the cartels, but it probably wouldn't be enough, counters Mazzitelli of the UNODC. "Legalization is a fake solution to the problem of security," he argues, citing a 2010 Rand Corp. report that found that legalizing marijuana in California would cut cartel profits by just 2 to 4 percent. If it does come, legalization is also quite a ways off—and Mexico's crisis is happening now. Only about half of U.S. citizens polled last year by Gallup supported legalizing marijuana, the least lucrative (and arguably the least dangerous) drug entering the country from Mexico.

If legalization is out and sending in the Army doesn't work, what's left? Among the most popular alternative ideas floating around Mexican civil society is that of creating "citizen security"—empowering local communities to resist organized crime. That means not only improving policing but also reintroducing the state in other ways, through education, economic opportunity, and a judicial system that investigates and punishes crime, explains Edgar Cortez, a researcher for the Mexican Institute of Human Rights and Democracy.

The broken justice system is unquestionably part of the problem. Mexico has a poor record of holding criminals to account for all manner of improper activity—from trafficking to homicide to regular old theft. "You have all these arrests and more than 40,000 deaths, but we don't have anybody arrested and investigated successfully," says McKay, the security consultant. Most police departments in the United States and Canada, he notes, have an 80 to 90 percent "solve rate" of finding the alleged perpetrator. "In Mexico it's almost zero." It's no coincidence that crime rates of almost every kind are up according to the Mexican government's own data. Extortion, bank robbery, kidnapping, and armed robbery have all risen dramatically since 2006.

The sheer amount of progress needed to stop the cartels is daunting. But Cantú, the human rights researcher, chooses to remain optimistic. "We have to put forward alternative options," he argues. "We have to call upon the people to have hope."

EVALUATING THE AUTHOR'S ARGUMENTS:

In this viewpoint Elizabeth Dickinson says that a drop in the cocaine trade through Mexico has been coupled with a rise in violence. What other drug-related explanation for this rise in violence would Paul Armentano, author of the preceding viewpoint, give?

Chapter 3

How Should Public Policy on Drugs Be Reformed?

FOR MEDICAL USE ONLY
as per A Health & y Code sections 11362.5 and 11362.7

The legalization of medical marijuana has become a hot-button issue in most states in America.

Marijuana Should Be Legalized for Medical Use

Gustin L. Reichbach

"When palliative care is understood as a fundamental human and medical right, marijuana for medical use should be beyond controversy."

In the following viewpoint Gustin L. Reichbach argues that legitimate clinical use of marijuana should be legalized. Reichbach gives a personal account of how marijuana helped alleviate his suffering from cancer and cancer treatment, contending that all patients like him should be allowed to legally use marijuana under a doctor's care. He claims that it is a medical and human rights issue. Reichbach was a justice of the New York State Supreme Court in Brooklyn prior to his death on July 14, 2012.

AS YOU READ, CONSIDER THE FOLLOWING QUESTIONS:

1. What three symptoms does Reichbach claim were alleviated by inhaled marijuana smoke?
2. What, according to the author, is the name of the oral synthetic substitute for inhaled marijuana?
3. According to Reichbach, how many states allow the legitimate clinical use of marijuana as of his writing?

Three and a half years ago, on my 62nd birthday, doctors discovered a mass on my pancreas. It turned out to be Stage 3 pancreatic cancer. I was told I would be dead in four to six months. Today I am in that rare coterie of people who have survived this long with the disease. But I did not foresee that after having dedicated myself for 40 years to a life of the law, including more than two decades as a New York State judge, my quest for ameliorative and palliative care would lead me to marijuana.

An Effective Medicine

My survival has demanded an enormous price, including months of chemotherapy, radiation hell and brutal surgery. For about a year, my cancer disappeared, only to return. About a month ago, I started a new and even more debilitating course of treatment. Every other week, after receiving an IV booster of chemotherapy drugs that takes three hours, I wear a pump that slowly injects more of the drugs over the next 48 hours.

> **FAST FACT**
>
> According to the *Syracuse Post-Standard*, a bill to legalize medical marijuana has passed the New York State Assembly three times: in 2007, 2008 and 2012, but has never even come to a vote in the Senate.

Nausea and pain are constant companions. One struggles to eat enough to stave off the dramatic weight loss that is part of this disease. Eating, one of the great pleasures of life, has now become a daily battle, with each forkful a small victory. Every drug prescribed to treat one problem leads to one or two more drugs to offset its side effects. Pain medication leads to loss of appetite and constipation. Anti-nausea medication raises glucose levels, a serious problem for me with my pancreas so compromised. Sleep, which might bring respite from the miseries of the day, becomes increasingly elusive.

Inhaled marijuana is the only medicine that gives me some relief from nausea, stimulates my appetite, and makes it easier to fall asleep. The oral synthetic substitute, Marinol, prescribed by my doctors, was useless. Rather than watch the agony of my suffering, friends have

Should doctors be allowed to prescribe marijuana for serious illnesses?

Taken from: CBS News poll, October 28–31, 2011.

chosen, at some personal risk, to provide the substance. I find a few puffs of marijuana before dinner gives me ammunition in the battle to eat. A few more puffs at bedtime permits desperately needed sleep.

A Medical and Human Rights Issue

This is not a law-and-order issue; it is a medical and a human rights issue. Being treated at Memorial Sloan Kettering Cancer Center, I am receiving the absolute gold standard of medical care. But doctors cannot be expected to do what the law prohibits, even when they know it is in the best interests of their patients. When palliative care is understood as a fundamental human and medical right, marijuana for medical use should be beyond controversy.

Sixteen states already permit the legitimate clinical use of marijuana, including our neighbor New Jersey, and Connecticut is on the cusp of becoming No. 17 [and did so on June 1, 2012]. The New York State Legislature is now debating a bill to recognize marijuana as an effective and legitimate medicinal substance and establish a lawful framework

A man smokes marijuana for medicinal purposes. Many cancer patients say smoking the drug helps overcome the pain, nausea, and appetite loss that accompany cancer treatment better than prescription drugs do.

for its use. The Assembly has passed such bills before, but they went nowhere in the State Senate. This year [2012] I hope that the outcome will be different. Cancer is a nonpartisan disease, so ubiquitous that it's impossible to imagine that there are legislators whose families have not also been touched by this scourge. It is to help all who have been affected by cancer, and those who will come after, that I now speak.

The Need to Legalize Medical Marijuana

Given my position as a sitting judge still hearing cases, well-meaning friends question the wisdom of my coming out on this issue. But I recognize that fellow cancer sufferers may be unable, for a host of reasons, to give voice to our plight. It is another heartbreaking aporia [contradiction] in the world of cancer that the one drug that gives relief without deleterious side effects remains classified as a narcotic with no medicinal value.

Because criminalizing an effective medical technique affects the fair administration of justice, I feel obliged to speak out as both a judge and a cancer patient suffering with a fatal disease. I implore the governor and the Legislature of New York, always considered a leader among states, to join the forward and humane thinking of 16 other states and pass the medical marijuana bill this year. Medical science has not yet found a cure, but it is barbaric to deny us access to one substance that has proved to ameliorate our suffering.

EVALUATING THE AUTHOR'S ARGUMENTS:

In this viewpoint Gustin L. Reichbach argues that the use of inhaled marijuana helped alleviate some of his suffering from cancer and cancer treatment. On its own, is his anecdote a compelling reason to legalize medical marijuana? Why or why not?

Marijuana Should Not Be Legalized for Medical Use

US Drug Enforcement Administration

"Science, not popular vote, should determine what medicine is."

In the following viewpoint the US Drug Enforcement Administration (DEA) argues that smoked marijuana has no documented medical value and is illegal under federal law and unapproved by the Food and Drug Administration (FDA). The DEA claims that neither voices from the medical community nor medical research supports the medical use of marijuana. However, the DEA does support ongoing research into the medical use of marijuana's ingredients. The DEA is the federal agency responsible for enforcing the controlled substances laws and regulations of the United States.

AS YOU READ, CONSIDER THE FOLLOWING QUESTIONS:

1. According to the DEA, in what case did the US Supreme Court decline to find an exception for medical marijuana use under the Controlled Substances Act?
2. The author claims that a 1999 study by what agency undermines the idea that smoked marijuana can be used as medicine?
3. According to the DEA, what is the only drug currently approved by the FDA that contains a synthetic form of a marijuana ingredient?

"The DEA Position on Marijuana," United States Drug Enforcement Agency (DEA), January 2011, pp. 3–6.

In 1970, Congress enacted laws against marijuana based in part on its conclusion that marijuana has no scientifically proven medical value. Likewise, the Food and Drug Administration (FDA), which is responsible for approving drugs as safe and effective medicine, has thus far declined to approve smoked marijuana for any condition or disease. Indeed, the FDA has noted that "there is currently sound evidence that smoked marijuana is harmful," and "that no sound scientific studies support medical use of marijuana for treatment in the United States, and no animal or human data support the safety or efficacy of marijuana for general medical use."

The Legal Status of Medical Marijuana

The United States Supreme Court has also declined to carve out an exception for marijuana under a theory of medical viability. In 2001, for example, the Supreme Court decided that a 'medical necessity' defense against prosecution was unavailable to defendants because Congress had purposely placed marijuana into Schedule I, which enumerates those controlled substances without any medical benefits.

In *Gonzales v. Raich* (2005), the Court had another opportunity to create a type of 'medical necessity' defense in a case involving severely ill California residents who had received physician approval to cultivate and use marijuana under California's Compassionate Use Act (CUA). Despite the state's attempt to shield its residents from liability under CUA, the Supreme Court held that Congress' power to regulate interstate drug markets included the authority to regulate wholly intrastate markets as well. Consequently, the Court again declined to carve out a 'medical necessity' defense, finding that the CSA [Controlled Substances Act] was not diminished in the face of any state law to the contrary and could support the specific enforcement actions at issue.

FAST FACT

Although seventeen states allow the medical use of marijuana, marijuana is still illegal under federal law; however, federal prosecutors have been instructed to target those engaged in cultivation and trafficking, not individuals using marijuana in compliance with state laws.

In a show of support for the *Raich* decision, the International Narcotics Control Board (INCB) issued this statement urging other countries to consider the real dangers of cannabis:

> Cannabis is classified under international conventions as a drug with a number of personal and public health problems. It is not a 'soft' drug as some people would have you believe. There is new evidence confirming well-known mental health problems, and some countries with a more liberal policy towards cannabis are reviewing their position. Countries need to take a strong stance towards cannabis abuse.

The Opinion of the Medical Community

The DEA and the federal government are not alone in viewing smoked marijuana as having no documented medical value. Voices in the medical community likewise do not accept smoked marijuana as medicine:

- The American Medical Association (AMA) has always endorsed "well-controlled studies of marijuana and related cannabinoids in patients with serious conditions for which preclinical, anecdotal, or controlled evidence suggests possible efficacy and the application of such results to the understanding and treatment of disease." In November 2009, the AMA amended its policy, urging that marijuana's status as a Schedule I controlled substance be reviewed "with the goal of facilitating the conduct of clinical research and development of cannabinoid-based medicines, and alternate delivery methods." The AMA also stated that "this should not be viewed as an endorsement of state-based medical cannabis programs, the legalization of marijuana, or that scientific evidence on the therapeutic use of cannabis meets the current standards for prescription drug product."

- The American Society of Addiction Medicine's (ASAM) public policy statement on "Medical Marijuana," clearly rejects smoking as a means of drug delivery. ASAM further recommends that "all cannabis, cannabis-based products and cannabis delivery devices should be subject to the same standards applicable to all other prescription medication and medical devices, and should not be distributed or otherwise provided to patients. . . ." without FDA approval. ASAM also "discourages state interference in the federal medication approval process."

- The American Cancer Society (ACS) "does not advocate inhaling smoke, nor the legalization of marijuana," although the organization does support carefully controlled clinical studies for alternative delivery methods, specifically a tetrahydrocannabinol (THC) skin patch.

- The American Glaucoma Society (AGS) has stated that "although marijuana can lower the intraocular pressure, the side effects and short duration of action, coupled with the lack of evidence that its use alters the course of glaucoma, preclude recommending this drug in any form for the treatment of glaucoma at the present time."

- The American Academy of Pediatrics (AAP) believes that "[a]ny change in the legal status of marijuana, even if limited to adults, could affect the prevalence of use among adolescents." While it supports scientific research on the possible medical use of cannabinoids as opposed to smoked marijuana, it opposes the legalization of marijuana.

- The National Multiple Sclerosis Society (NMSS) has stated that it could not recommend medical marijuana be made widely available for people with multiple sclerosis for symptom management, explaining: "This decision was not only based on existing legal barriers to its use but, even more importantly, because studies to date do not demonstrate a clear benefit compared to existing symptomatic therapies and because side effects, systemic effects, and long-term effects are not yet clear."
- The British Medical Association (BMA) voiced extreme concern that downgrading the criminal status of marijuana would "mislead" the public into believing that the drug is safe. The BMA maintains that marijuana "has been linked to greater risk of heart disease, lung cancer, bronchitis and emphysema." The 2004 Deputy Chairman of the BMA's Board of Science said that "[t]he public must be made aware of the harmful effects we know result from smoking this drug."

The Medical Properties of Marijuana

In 1999, The Institute of Medicine (IOM) released a landmark study reviewing the supposed medical properties of marijuana. The study is frequently cited by "medical" marijuana advocates, but in fact severely undermines their arguments.

- After release of the IOM study, the principal investigators cautioned that the active compounds in marijuana may have medicinal potential and therefore should be researched further. However, the study concluded that "there is little future in smoked marijuana as a medically approved medication."
- For some ailments, the IOM found ". . . potential therapeutic value of cannabinoid drugs, primarily THC, for pain relief, control of nausea and vomiting, and appetite stimulation." However, it pointed out that "[t]he effects of cannabinoids on the symptoms studied are generally modest, and in most cases there are more effective medications [than smoked marijuana]."
- The study concluded that, at best, there is only anecdotal information on the medical benefits of smoked marijuana for some ailments, such as muscle spasticity. For other ailments, such as epilepsy and glaucoma, the study found no evidence of medical value and did not endorse further research.

- The IOM study explained that "smoked marijuana . . . is a crude THC delivery system that also delivers harmful substances." In addition, "plants contain a variable mixture of biologically active compounds and cannot be expected to provide a precisely defined drug effect." Therefore, the study concluded that "there is little future in smoked marijuana as a medically approved medication."
- The principal investigators explicitly stated that using smoked marijuana in clinical trials "should not be designed to develop it as a licensed drug, but should be a stepping stone to the development of new, safe delivery systems of cannabinoids."

Police and DEA officers raid a medical marijuana dispensary in San Francisco. Although California and many other states allow the medical use of marijuana, federal laws still hold such use to be a criminal offense.

Thus, even scientists and researchers who believe that certain active ingredients in marijuana may have potential medicinal value openly *discount the notion that smoked marijuana is or can become "medicine."*

Potential Medicinal Uses of Marijuana's Ingredients

The Drug Enforcement Administration supports ongoing research into potential medicinal uses of marijuana's active ingredients. As of December 2010:

- There are 111 researchers registered with DEA to perform studies with marijuana, marijuana extracts, and non-tetrahydrocannabinol marijuana derivatives that exist in the plant, such as cannabidiol and cannabinol.
- Studies include evaluation of abuse potential, physical/psychological effects, adverse effects, therapeutic potential, and detection.
- Fourteen of the researchers are approved to conduct research with smoked marijuana on human subjects.

At present, however, *the clear weight of the evidence is that smoked marijuana is harmful.* No matter what medical condition has been studied, other drugs already approved by the FDA have been proven to be safer than smoked marijuana.

The only drug currently approved by the FDA that contains the synthetic form of THC is Marinol®. Available through prescription, Marinol® comes in pill form, and is used to relieve nausea and vomiting associated with chemotherapy for cancer patients and to assist with loss of appetite with AIDS patients.

Sativex®, an oromucosal spray for the treatment of spasticity due to Multiple Sclerosis, is already approved for use in Canada and was approved in June 2010 for use in the United Kingdom. The oral liquid spray contains two of the cannabinoids found in marijuana—THC and cannabidiol (CBD)—but unlike smoked marijuana, removes contaminants, reduces the intoxicating effects, is grown in a structured and scientific environment, administers a set dosage and meets criteria for pharmaceutical products.

Organizers behind the "medical" marijuana movement have not dealt with ensuring that the product meets the standards of modern medicine: quality, safety and efficacy. There is no standardized composition or dosage; no appropriate prescribing information; no quality control; no accountability for the product; no safety regulation; no way to measure its effectiveness (besides anecdotal stories); and no insurance coverage. Science, not popular vote, should determine what medicine is.

EVALUATING THE AUTHOR'S ARGUMENTS:

In this viewpoint the US Drug Enforcement Administration claims that smoked marijuana is harmful and thus should not be used as medicine. How might Gustin L. Reichbach, author of the previous viewpoint, respond to this assertion? Whose argument do you agree more with? Why?

Marijuana Should Be Regulated in the Same Manner as Alcohol

Pete Holmes

"Marijuana is far more like alcohol than it is like hard drugs, and we should treat it as such."

In the following viewpoint Pete Holmes argues that marijuana should be regulated and taxed, just like alcohol. Holmes claims that marijuana prohibition inhibits effective prevention of risk and harm and undermines respect for the law. Holmes proposes legalizing personal use of marijuana and small-scale production as a way to improve public safety and efficient government spending. Holmes is Seattle city attorney.

AS YOU READ, CONSIDER THE FOLLOWING QUESTIONS:

1. What four examples does Holmes give in support of his view that regulation is preferable to prohibition?
2. The author cites a quote by Albert Einstein in order to draw an analogy between what two prohibitions?
3. Does Holmes believe Washington should wait for the federal government to legalize marijuana use before passing a state law?

Marijuana prohibition is more than a practical failure; it has been a misuse of both taxpayer dollars and the government's authority over the people.

An Alternative to Prohibition

As the steward of reduced prosecutorial dollars, I am the first Seattle city attorney to stop prosecuting marijuana-possession cases and to call for the legalization, taxation and regulation of marijuana for adult recreational use.

We have long since agreed as a society that substances should not be prohibited by the government simply because they can be harmful if misused or consumed in excess. Alcohol, food and cars can all be extremely dangerous under certain circumstances, and cigarettes are almost always harmful in the long term. All these things kill many people every year.

But we don't try to ban any of them—because we can't, and we don't need to. Instead, we regulate their manufacture and use, we tax them, and we encourage those who choose to use them to do so in as safe a manner as possible.

A member of the Green Hope Patient Network, a medical marijuana advocacy group, displays a letter from the state of Washington stating that medical marijuana is now subject to state sales tax. Many believe that taxing and regulating marijuana is a step in the right direction.

STATE OF WASHINGTON
DEPARTMENT OF REVENUE

December 10, 2010

Green Hope Patient Network
Suite 106
1207 N 200th St
Shoreline WA 98133-3213

SUBJECT: SALES TAX ON MEDICAL MARIJUANA

The Department of Revenue has recently published a *Tax Top* treatment on sales of medical marijuana.

Sales tax must be collected and remitted
Medical marijuana sales to consumers in Washington State **marijuana dispensaries are required to collect and rem** *addition,* the dispensaries are subject to the business and retailing classification on these sales.

Medical

Marijuana is far more like alcohol than it is like hard drugs, and we should treat it as such. We address alcohol abuse primarily as a public-health issue, and we should do the same with marijuana abuse. Inebriation only becomes a crime for those who choose to get behind the wheel, whether the intoxicant is alcohol, prescription pain killers or cannabis.

The Right Regulations

My focus as city attorney is to ensure that we have ways to regulate the production and distribution of any potentially harmful substance so that we limit the potential risk and harm. Outright prohibition is an ineffective means of doing this.

Instead, I support tightening laws against driving while stoned, preventing the sale of marijuana to minors, and ensuring that anything other than small-scale noncommercial marijuana production takes place in regulated agricultural facilities—and not residential basements.

It is critical that we get these details right. Ending marijuana prohibition isn't a panacea, but it's a necessary step in the right direction, and the specifics of a rational regulatory system for marijuana are important.

Ending marijuana prohibition is pro–law enforcement because it would enhance the legitimacy of our laws and law enforcement. As [physicist] Albert Einstein said of Prohibition in 1921, "Nothing is more destructive of respect for the government and the law of the land than passing laws which cannot be enforced."

Marijuana prohibition cannot be and has not been consistently enforced, and keeping it on the books diminishes the people's respect for law enforcement.

> **FAST FACT**
>
> Washington's HB 1550— the bill to legalize marijuana—died in committee in April 2012, but Washington voters in November 2012 approved marijuana legalization under Initiative 502.

The Need for State Legalization of Marijuana

I applaud the state Legislature for recently holding a hearing on House Bill 1550, which would legalize marijuana. This is an important start

Support for Making Use of Marijuana Legal

Do you think the use of marijuana should be made legal or not?

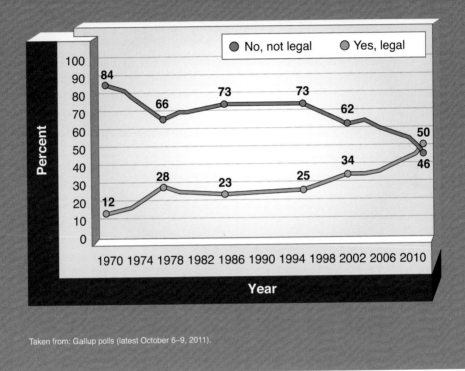

Taken from: Gallup polls (latest October 6–9, 2011).

to the conversation about ending prohibition, which I believe is likely to lead to a successful citizens' initiative if the Legislature doesn't step up and do the right thing first.

Ending marijuana prohibition and focusing on rational regulation and taxation is a pro–public safety, pro–public health, pro–limited government policy. I urge the state Legislature to move down this road.

Even if marijuana remains illegal under federal law, it is still time for Washington state to act. As with alcohol prohibition, collective action by the states will help us end the federal marijuana prohibition and transition to a rational and functional system for regulating and taxing marijuana.

The state of Washington should not use the continued existence of the federal prohibition as an excuse for leaving our misguided and wasteful state prohibition system in place.

EVALUATING THE AUTHOR'S ARGUMENTS:

In this viewpoint Pete Holmes claims that marijuana and alcohol are similar enough to be treated the same under the law. How might an opponent of this view argue that the two substances are dissimilar in a way that requires different treatment under the law?

California Voters Should Reject Legalizing Marijuana

"Evidence, reason, and values should dissuade people from the legalization pipe dream."

The Christian Science Monitor

In the following viewpoint the *Christian Science Monitor* argues that marijuana should not be legalized. Considering the arguments in favor of legalization, the *Christian Science Monitor* denies that marijuana legalization in California would hinder drug trafficking by cartels and denies that legalization would have much of a positive fiscal impact. The *Monitor* contends that the health and public-safety dangers of marijuana legalization support continued prohibition. The *Christian Science Monitor* is a national newspaper.

AS YOU READ, CONSIDER THE FOLLOWING QUESTIONS:

1. According to the author, how does the proposal in California's Proposition 19 differ from the legal treatment of marijuana in the Netherlands?
2. Approximately what percentage of the drug cartels' money comes from marijuana trafficked to the United States, according to the *Monitor*?
3. According to the author, what percentage of marijuana users aged eighteen or older are either dependent on the drug or abuse it?

*P*roposition 19 would make California the first state to fully legalize marijuana. Supporters sound persuasive with talk about weakening Mexican drug cartels and helping state revenues with taxes on pot. But their arguments don't hold up.

California voters are considering a ballot measure that would make their state the first jurisdiction in the nation—and the world—to fully legalize marijuana.

This is not a "first" that voters should support.

Proposition 19 would legalize marijuana for recreational use for people ages 21 and older. It would also allow local governments to tax and regulate commercial production and distribution—not just retail sale, as in the Netherlands.

Proponents argue that treating pot like alcohol and tobacco will increase revenues for the cash-strapped state and decrease violence and the profits of the Mexican drug cartels. All along, supporters of legalization have maintained that pot is harmless.

FAST FACT

After the failure of Proposition 19 in California in 2010, three proposed initiatives for marijuana legalization in California failed to gather enough signatures for the 2012 election.

Whether Californians are buying this sales pitch is unclear. A September Field poll finds that 49 percent of likely voters say they're inclined to support Proposition 19 and legalization, while 42 percent are inclined to oppose it. A Reuters/Ipsos poll released Oct. 5 shows the opposite: 53 percent of voters are against it.

Evidence, reason, and values should dissuade people from the legalization pipe dream. Here's a look at why the arguments of the well-funded "pro" side don't hold up:

Not much impact on drug cartels. Legalizing marijuana in California "would not appreciably influence the Mexican drug trafficking organizations and the related violence," according to Beau Kilmer, lead author of a report released this month by the RAND Corporation.

This nonprofit research organization has published independent studies this year that look at the potential effects of legalizing pot in California.

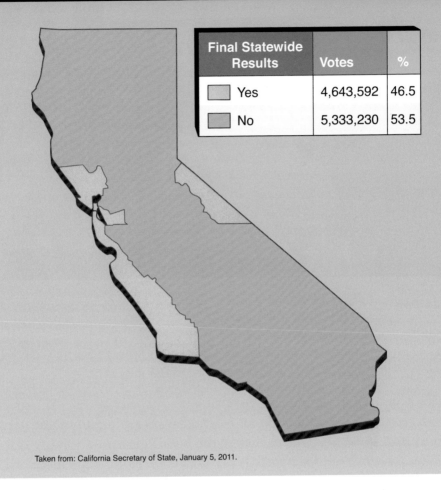

Proposition 19 Results, November 2, 2010, to Legalize, Regulate, and Tax Marijuana in California

Final Statewide Results	Votes	%
☐ Yes	4,643,592	46.5
☐ No	5,333,230	53.5

Taken from: California Secretary of State, January 5, 2011.

RAND found that marijuana exports to the United States do not account for 60 percent of drug cartel revenues from exports, as is often reported. Rather, the cartels get only 15 to 26 percent of their money from pot trafficked to the US.

If California, which accounts for one-seventh of pot use nationwide, goes legal, total drug export revenues for the cartels will drop by "perhaps 2 to 4 percent." The big money—and the big violence—is in harder drugs.

RAND did acknowledge an exception. If high-potency California marijuana is smuggled to other states at low prices, it could seriously

California's Proposition 19, a proposal to fully legalize marijuana and tax it, failed to pass in a 2010 vote.

eat into the cartels' take—cutting out roughly 20 percent of total export drug money.

Still, many factors could deter smuggling (and state legalization itself), including the federal government. Any use or sale of marijuana is a criminal offense under federal law. Washington might step in to stop smuggling, or challenge the ballot measure's legality if it passes, or withhold federal highway dollars for noncompliance with the federal law.

Don't count on tax revenues. Pot supporters say California could reap $1.4 billion from marijuana taxes, citing an estimate by the Board of Equalization, which administers the state sales tax.

But the board assumes a $50-an-ounce tax—a rate mentioned nowhere in the proposition and one that could be easily undercut by a black market. That's what happened in the 1990s in Canada with a mere $3 tax on cigarettes. The tax had to be repealed.

Tax evasion could be widespread, and because taxing is left up to local jurisdictions, even the potential amounts will vary. If one jurisdiction opts for a low tax rate, and the marijuana industry moves to that place, then other jurisdictions won't collect much.

RAND again steps in as a leveler when talking about savings from the criminal justice system: $1 billion saved? More like $300 million, and that doesn't account for the social costs associated with increased pot use and dependence. RAND predicts legalization will push marijuana prices down by as much as 80 percent, spurring greater use, especially among younger people.

The White House drug czar reported Thursday that overall marijuana use increased sharply—by 9 percent—from 2008 to '09. Over the same time period, kids started using pot at a younger age. The average age for first use dropped from 17.8 years to 17. Increasing societal acceptance of marijuana is one reason behind these trends.

Pot is harmful. More than 30 percent of people who are 18 and older and who used marijuana in the past year are either dependent on the drug or abuse it, according to a 2004 study in the *Journal of the American Medical Association.*

Pot is associated with cognitive impairment (affecting the ability to think, reason, and process information), poor motor skills, and respiratory and mental illness.

Critics of Prop. 19 are alarmed that its wording will affect traffic safety. The measure prohibits smoking pot while operating a vehicle, but "there is nothing to prevent drivers from smoking just prior to getting behind the wheel," writes Pete Dunbar, former deputy police chief in Oakland.

If the ballot measure is defeated, supporters will likely regroup for another day, and try to fix flaws in the measure.

But no amount of redrafting can counter the moral argument against legalization: Real joy and satisfaction are not found in a drug. You don't advance social good by making it easier for people to get high.

EVALUATING THE AUTHOR'S ARGUMENTS:

In this viewpoint the *The Christian Science Monitor* disputes the arguments in favor of treating marijuana like alcohol. Do any of the author's arguments against legalization of marijuana also apply to alcohol? Explain.

Current Drug Prohibition Laws Should Be Repealed

Jacob Sullum

"If illegality is the problem, legality is the solution."

In the following viewpoint Jacob Sullum argues that the war on drugs has failed and that ending it will require the legalization of all intoxicants. Sullum claims that criticism of the global war on drugs is mounting; however, he denies that anything less than full legalization will solve the many problems of prohibition, claiming that decriminalizing possession while criminalizing production makes no sense. Sullum is a senior editor at *Reason* magazine and Reason.com and author of *Saying Yes: In Defense of Drug Use.*

AS YOU READ, CONSIDER THE FOLLOWING QUESTIONS:

1. According to the author, which government official claims that the drug war ended in 2009?
2. The presidents of which three Latin American countries recently criticized the global war on drugs, according to Sullum?
3. According to Sullum, what effect of prohibition makes drug use more dangerous than it would otherwise be?

Forty years ago this Friday [Friday 17, 2011], President Richard Nixon announced that "public enemy number one in the United States is drug abuse." Declaring that "the problem has assumed the dimensions of a national emergency," he asked Congress for money to "wage a new, all-out offensive," a crusade he would later call a "global war on the drug menace."

The War on Drugs

The war on drugs ended in May 2009, when President [Barack] Obama's newly appointed drug czar, Gil Kerlikowske, said he planned

Drug czar Gil Kerlikowske (pictured) in 2009 declared the war on drugs over, but the federal government has not moved to decriminalize or legalize any illegal drugs.

to stop calling it that. Or so Kerlikowske claims. "We certainly ended the drug war now almost two years ago," he told Seattle's PBS station last March [2011], "in the first interview that I did.". . .

In reality, of course, Richard Nixon did not start the war on drugs, and Barack Obama, who in 2004 called it "an utter failure," did not end it. The war on drugs will continue as long as the government insists on getting between people and the intoxicants they want. And while it is heartening to hear a growing chorus of prominent critics decry the enormous collateral damage caused by this policy, few seem prepared to give peace a chance by renouncing the use of force to impose arbitrary pharmacological preferences.

Criticism of the Global War on Drugs

"The global war on drugs has failed, with devastating consequences for individuals and societies around the world," a recent report from the Global Commission on Drug Policy concludes. "Political leaders and public figures should have the courage to articulate publicly what many of them acknowledge privately: that the evidence overwhelmingly demonstrates that repressive strategies will not solve the drug problem, and that the war on drugs has not, and cannot, be won."

Each year that we fail to face this reality, the report says, "billions of dollars are wasted on ineffective programs," "millions of citizens are sent to prison unnecessarily," and "hundreds of thousands of people die from preventable overdoses and diseases."

This strong criticism of the status quo was endorsed by the three former Latin American presidents who organized the commission—Fernando Henrique Cardoso of Brazil, César Gaviria of Colombia, and Ernesto Zedillo of Mexico—and 16 other notable names, including former Secretary of State George Shultz, former Federal Reserve Chairman Paul Volcker, Greek Prime Minister George Papandreou, former U.N. Secretary

> **FAST FACT**
>
> According to the Federal Bureau of Investigation, in 2008 there were 1,702,537 arrests for drug law violations, and in 2010 there were 1,638,846 such arrests.

The term *war on drugs* has been used to describe the efforts of the US government to reduce the illegal drug trade. From what you have seen, read, or heard, would you describe the war on drugs as a success or a failure?

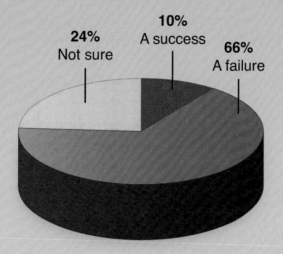

24%
Not sure

10%
A success

66%
A failure

Taken from: Angus Reid Public Opinion Survey, May 29–30, 2012. www.angus-reid.com.

General Kofi Annan, former NATO Secretary General Javier Solana, Peruvian novelist Mario Vargas Llosa, and Virgin Group founder Richard Branson.

The Need to End Prohibition

The alternatives suggested by the commission are less impressive. The report calls for easing up on drug users and low-level participants in the drug trade while cracking down on "violent criminal organizations." But it is prohibition that enriches and empowers such organizations while encouraging them to be violent—a point the commission acknowledges. As a new report from Law Enforcement Against Prohibition notes regarding the escalating violence that has left some 40,000 people dead since Mexican President Felipe Calderon began an anti-drug crackdown in 2006, "this is a cycle that cannot and will not end until prohibition itself ends."

It is also prohibition that breeds official corruption, makes drug use more dangerous than it would otherwise be, and undermines civil liberties—all problems the commission highlights. Furthermore, a policy of decriminalizing possession while maintaining the bans on production and sale is morally incoherent: If drug use itself is not worthy of punishment, why should people go to prison merely for helping others commit this noncrime?

In a recent *Wall Street Journal* op-ed piece, Shultz and Volcker liken the war on drugs to alcohol prohibition, approvingly quote [economist] Milton Friedman's argument that "illegality creates obscene profits that finance the murderous tactics of the drug lords" and "leads to the corruption of law enforcement officials," and then recoil in horror from the logical conclusion, saying "we do not support the simple legalization of all drugs." If illegality is the problem, legality is the solution.

EVALUATING THE AUTHOR'S ARGUMENTS:

In this viewpoint Jacob Sullum says that it is incoherent to punish drug producers without punishing users. How might a proponent of this view argue that such a policy is coherent?

Legalizing Drugs Isn't the Answer

Margaret Wente

"If the only alternative to the war on drugs were legalization, then legalization would look good. But there are many other things we can do to minimize the impact of illegal drugs."

In the following viewpoint Margaret Wente argues that drug legalization is not the answer to the problems with current drug policy. Wente claims that although the idea of drug legalization is popular, the reality would be a big mistake. Citing the research of a public policy expert, Wente contends that drug legalization would create increased consumption and public health problems. Wente concludes that there are alternatives to the current drug war that are more promising than repealing prohibition. Wente is a columnist for Canada's largest national daily newspaper, Toronto's *Globe and Mail*.

Most of us can agree that current drug policy in North America is a disaster. The global war on drugs can't be won. Locking up addicts in jail is both futile and inhumane. We're squandering billions on policies that hurt people and don't work.

So it's no wonder that the idea of legalizing drugs is more popular than ever. Half of all Americans believe marijuana should be legalized, according to a recent survey. The California Medical Association has come out in favour of it. Social progressives aren't the only ones who argue that drug laws should be repealed. Libertarians think so, too. As Thunder Bay Mayor Keith Hobbs puts it, "Look at the money that governments make off alcohol. You know, perhaps instead of organized crime getting the profits [from marijuana] the federal government could generate revenues from it." Neil Reynolds, writing in this space the other day argued that we should legalize most hard drugs as well. After all, drugs can't possibly hurt society as much as prohibition does.

FAST FACT

Bills aimed at decriminalizing marijuana possession for personal use in Canada failed in the Canadian Parliament in both 2002 and 2004.

These arguments drive Mark Kleiman crazy. Mr. Kleiman, a professor of public policy at UCLA, knows as much about this subject as anyone on the planet. His politics are liberal. He, too, thinks our current policies are a disaster. But he also thinks the legalizers are just as misguided as the hard-liners with their fantasies of a drug-free world. His information-packed new book, *Drugs and Drug Policy*, is full of inconvenient facts that demolish both the hawks and the doves.

Mr. Kleiman maintains that legalizing drugs would create far bigger problems than the legalizers think. Consider alcohol and tobacco, which are heavily taxed and regulated, and are the focus of massive public health campaigns. Even so, both are associated with major public health disasters. Alcohol alone kills more than 100,000 people a year in North America—more than all illicit drugs combined.

Both the booze industry and the tobacco industry depend on heavy users for their profits. That's because those people account for the lion's share of consumption. The alcohol industry, for example, gets 80 per cent of its revenue from people with drinking problems. As Mr. Kleiman says, "To the consumer, developing a bad habit is bad news. To the marketing executive, it's the whole point of the exercise." It's not hard to imagine what full-scale commercialization would do to marijuana. "It would vastly increase the cannabis-abuse problem by giving the marketing geniuses who have done such a

Opponents of medical marijuana legalization say it will only increase consumption and abuse.

Canadian Opinion on Marijuana Law Reform

Opinion	Percent
Legalize/decriminalize	66
It should be legalized and taxed	40
It should be decriminalized for small amounts	26
The law should be left as is	20
Penalties should be increased	11
Do not know	2

Taken from: Forum Research Inc. poll, December 13, 2011. Ian Vandaelle. "Majority of Canadians Support Legalizing or Decriminalizing Marijuana, New Poll Suggests." *National Post,* January 17, 2012.

fine job persuading children to smoke tobacco, drink to excess and supersize themselves with junk food another vice to foster."

Then there's basic economics. When you legalize a prohibited substance, the price usually drops. The result is a big increase in consumption, along with problem users. (If you try to keep the price high through taxes, you'll just create a big black market.) And although marijuana on the whole is probably less destructive than alcohol, it is by no means harmless. Just ask the parents of any 15-year-old who's developed a taste for weed.

Mr. Kleiman points out that, in many ways, marijuana is a red herring in the drug debate. Although it accounts for the vast majority of illegal drug users, it accounts for only a fraction of illegal revenue. He favours a limited form of legalization that would allow individuals and small non-profit groups to grow and trade their own.

But marijuana isn't our real drug problem. Legalizing it would have very little impact on the global drug trade or on violent crime. As for cocaine and heroin, if we ever did legalize them (unlikely, given public sentiment), we could well discover we'd just doubled the size of the market without driving the crime rate down.

If the only alternative to the war on drugs were legalization, then legalization would look good. But there are many other things we can do to minimize the impact of illegal drugs. We can have law enforcement focus on public safety, not busting users. We can adopt promising new programs that get addicts on parole to kick the habit. We can do far more to intervene early with people who have addiction problems. It's even possible that we could have most of the benefits of prohibition at a smaller fraction of the cost—once we stop yelling at each other.

EVALUATING THE AUTHOR'S ARGUMENTS:

In this viewpoint Margaret Wente claims that drugs should not be legalized but that law enforcement should not punish drug users either. What would Jacob Sullum, author of the previous viewpoint, say about this proposal?

Facts About Drug Legalization

Editor's note: These facts can be used in reports to add credibility when making important points or claims.

Legal Status of Drugs in the United States

- The Controlled Substances Act (CSA) was enacted into law by the Congress of the United States in 1970, under which the manufacture, importation, possession, use, and distribution of certain substances is regulated.
- Drugs classified as Schedule I controlled substances under the CSA are defined as having a high potential for abuse and no currently accepted medical use. They include heroin, LSD, marijuana, MDMA (ecstasy), and peyote, and are not legal under any circumstances.
- Drugs classified as Schedule II controlled substances under the CSA are defined as having a high potential for abuse and certain accepted medical uses. They include cocaine, methadone, methamphetamine, morphine, and PCP, and are legal if used for medical purposes and prescribed by a medical doctor.
- Drugs classified as Schedule III controlled substances under the CSA are defined as having accepted medical uses and a small to moderate chance of dependence. They include such prescription drugs as codeine and steroids and are legal if used for medical purposes and prescribed by a medical doctor.
- Drugs classified as Schedule IV controlled substances under the CSA are defined as having accepted medical uses and limited possibilities of dependence. They include such prescription drugs as Valium and Xanax and are legal if used for medical purposes and prescribed by a medical doctor.
- Drugs classified as Schedule V controlled substances under the CSA are defined as having accepted medical uses and the lowest possibility of dependence. They include over-the-counter drugs such as cough medicine and are legal if used for medical purposes.

- As of November 2012, fifteen states—Alaska, Arizona, California, Connecticut, Delaware, Hawaii, Maine, Michigan, Montana, Nevada, New Jersey, New Mexico, Oregon, Rhode Island, and Vermont—and the District of Columbia have passed legislation that decriminalizes the use of medical marijuana, while Colorado and Washington have legalized marijuana for nonmedical use as well.
- Although state laws allowing medical marijuana exempt patients and physicians from prosecution for violating state laws, the state laws do not protect them from federal criminal prosecution under the CSA for production, distribution, and possession.

The War on Drugs

- The war on drugs began in 1971, when President Richard Nixon said, "America's public enemy number one in the United States is drug abuse. In order to fight and defeat this enemy, it is necessary to wage a new, all-out offensive."
- The Drug Enforcement Administration (DEA) is the agency within the US Department of Justice tasked with preventing drug smuggling into the country and stopping drug production, distribution, and use within the country.

According to the DEA:

- In 1972, the first full year of the war on drugs, the DEA employed 2,775 people with a budget of $65,200,000;
- forty years later, in 2012, the DEA employs 9,539 people with a budget of $2,035,000,000.

According to the Federal Bureau of Investigation:
- In 2010 there were 1,638,846 drug arrests;
- approximately half of the drug arrests, 853,839, were for marijuana.

Illicit Drug Use in the United States

According to the 2011 National Survey on Drug Use and Health (NSDUH):

- 8.7 percent of the population aged twelve or older reported past-month use of an illicit drug;

- 10.1 percent of youths aged twelve to seventeen reported past-month use of an illicit drug;
- 21.4 percent of young adults aged eighteen to twenty-five reported past-month use of an illicit drug;
- 18.1 million Americans aged twelve or older reported past-month marijuana use;
- an estimated 6.5 million people aged twelve or older were classified with substance dependence or abuse of illicit drugs.

Public Opinion on Drug Legalization

According to a 2012 poll by Angus Reid:

- 68 percent of Americans believe the country has a serious drug abuse problem that affects the whole country, and 20 percent believe there is a drug abuse problem but that it is confined to specific areas and people;
- 66 percent think the war on drugs has been a failure, 10 percent think it has been a success, and 24 percent are not sure;
- 52 percent support the legalization of marijuana;
- 9 percent support the legalization of cocaine;
- 8 percent support the legalization of heroin;
- 7 percent support the legalization of methamphetamine.

Organizations to Contact

The editors have compiled the following list of organizations concerned with the issues debated in this book. The descriptions are derived from materials provided by the organizations. All have publications or information available for interested readers. The list was compiled on the date of publication of the present volume; the information provided here may change. Be aware that many organizations take several weeks or longer to respond to inquiries, so allow as much time as possible for the receipt of requested materials.

American Civil Liberties Union (ACLU)
125 Broad St., 18th Fl., New York, NY 10004
(212) 549-2500
e-mail: aclu@aclu.org
website: www.aclu.org

The ACLU is a national organization that works to defend Americans' civil rights guaranteed by the US Constitution by providing legal defense, research, and education. The ACLU opposes the criminal prohibition of marijuana. The ACLU Drug Law Reform Project engages in campaigns and submits briefs in relevant law cases, with literature about these campaigns and text of the briefs available at the ACLU website.

American Council for Drug Education (ACDE)
50 Jay St., Brooklyn, NY 11201
(646) 505-2061
e-mail: acde@phoenixhouse.org
website: www.acde.org

The ACDE seeks to diminish substance abuse. It creates accessible materials on the most current scientific research to those seeking accurate, compelling information on drugs. ACDE has resources about drug and alcohol abuse for parents, youth, educators, prevention professionals, employers, health-care professionals, and other concerned community members, including fact sheets on numerous substances.

Cato Institute
1000 Massachusetts Ave. NW, Washington, DC 20001-5403
(202) 842-0200 • fax: (202) 842-3490
e-mail: cato@cato.org
website: www.cato.org
The Cato Institute is a public policy research foundation dedicated to limiting the control of government and to protecting individual liberty. The Cato Institute strongly favors drug legalization. The institute publishes the *Cato Journal* three times a year and the *Cato Policy Report* bimonthly.

Drug Free America Foundation, Inc. (DFAF)
5999 Central Ave., Ste. 301, Saint Petersburg, FL 33710
(727) 828-0211 • fax: (727) 828-0212
website: www.dfaf.org
The DFAF is a drug prevention and policy organization committed to developing, promoting, and sustaining global strategies, policies, and laws that will reduce illegal drug use, drug addiction, drug-related injury, and death. It opposes efforts that would legalize, decriminalize, or promote illicit drugs. The DFAF publishes several position statements available at its website, including "Student Drug Testing Is Part of the Solution."

Drug Policy Alliance (DPA)
131 W. Thirty-Third St., 15th Fl., New York, NY 10001
(212) 613-8020 • fax: (212) 613-8021
e-mail: nyc@drugpolicy.org
website: www.drugpolicy.org
The DPA supports alternatives to current drug policy that are grounded in science, compassion, health, and human rights. It advances policies that reduce the harms of both drug use and drug prohibition and seek solutions that promote safety while upholding the sovereignty of individuals over their own minds and bodies. Among the DPA's recent publications is the booklet for parents *Safety First: A Reality-Based Approach to Teens and Drugs.*

Marijuana Policy Project (MPP)
236 Massachusetts Ave. NE, Ste. 400, Washington, DC 20002
(202) 462-5747
e-mail: info@mpp.org
website: www.mpp.org

The MPP works to further public policies that allow for responsible medical and nonmedical use of marijuana and that minimize the harms associated with marijuana consumption and the laws that manage its use. The MPP works to increase public awareness through speaking engagements, educational seminars, the mass media, and briefing papers and to increase public support for marijuana regulation. It lobbies for marijuana policy reform at the state and federal levels.

National Center on Addiction and Substance Abuse at Columbia University (CASA)
633 Third Ave., 19th Fl., New York, NY 10017-6706
(212) 841-5200
website: www.casacolumbia.org

CASA is a private nonprofit organization that aims to inform Americans of the economic and social costs of substance abuse and its impact on their lives, while also removing the stigma of substance abuse and replacing shame and despair with hope. The organization supports treatment as the best way to reduce chemical dependency. CASA publishes numerous reports and books, including *The Importance of Family Dinners VII.*

National Institute on Drug Abuse (NIDA)
Office of Science Policy and Communications, Public Information and Liaison Branch
6001 Executive Blvd., Rm. 5213, MSC 9561, Bethesda, MD 20892-9561
(301) 443-1124
e-mail: information@nida.nih.gov
website: www.nida.nih.gov

NIDA aims to bring the power of science to bear on drug abuse and addiction. It supports and conducts research on drug abuse—including the yearly Monitoring the Future Survey—to improve addiction prevention, treatment, and policy efforts. NIDA also publishes the bimonthly

NIDA Notes newsletter, the periodic *NIDA Capsules* fact sheets, and a catalog of research reports and public education materials, such as *Drugs: Shatter the Myths*.

National Organization for the Reform of Marijuana Laws (NORML)

1600 K St. NW, Mezzanine Level, Washington, DC 20006-2832
(202) 483-5500 • fax: (202) 483-0057
e-mail: norml@norml.org
website: www.norml.org

NORML works to move public opinion to achieve the repeal of marijuana prohibition so that the responsible use of cannabis by adults is no longer subject to penalty. It serves as an informational resource on marijuana-related topics and lobbies state and federal legislators to support reform legislation. NORML has numerous research and position papers available at its website, including *Real World Ramifications of Cannabis Legalization and Decriminalization.*

Office of National Drug Control Policy (ONDCP)

Drug Policy Information Clearinghouse, PO Box 6000
Rockville, MD 20849-6000
(800) 666-3332
website: www.whitehouse.gov/ondcp

The ONDCP, a component of the Executive Office of the President, establishes policies, priorities, and objectives for the nation's drug control program. The ONDCP coordinates drug-control activities and produces the annual National Drug Control Strategy, which outlines the administration's efforts to reduce illicit drug use, manufacturing, and trafficking; drug-related crime and violence; and drug-related health consequences. The ONDCP has numerous publications related to its mission, including the annual National Survey on Drug Use and Health.

The Partnership for a Drug-Free America

352 Park Ave. South, 9th Fl., New York, NY 10010
(212) 922-1560 • fax: (212) 922-1570
website: www.drugfree.org

The Partnership for a Drug-Free America is a nonprofit organization that works to help parents prevent, intervene in, or find treatment for drug and alcohol use by their children. The partnership offers information, tools, and opportunities to connect with other parents and caregivers who may have a child struggling with addiction. Its website features interactive tools that translate the latest science and research on teen behavior, addiction, and treatment into tips and tools for parents.

Rand Corporation
1776 Main St., Santa Monica, CA 90401-3208
(310) 393-0411 • fax: (310) 393-4818
website: www.rand.org

The Rand Corporation is a nonprofit institution that helps improve policy and decision making through research and analysis. The corporation's Drug Policy Research Center conducts research to help decision makers in the United States and throughout the world address issues involving alcohol and other drugs. The Drug Policy Research Center publishes research, available at its website, including "Marijuana Legalization: What Everyone Needs to Know."

For Further Reading

Books

Benavie, Arthur. *Drugs: America's Holy War.* New York: Routledge, 2009. Argues that an end to the war on drugs would yield enormous benefits, destroy dangerous drug cartels, and allow the government to refocus its attention on public health.

Chapkis, Wendy, and Richard J. Webb. *Dying to Get High: Marijuana as Medicine.* New York: New York University Press, 2008. Through interviews with patients, public officials, law enforcement officers, and physicians, chronicles the complex history of medical marijuana in America.

Earlywine, Mitch, ed. *Pot Politics: Marijuana, and the Costs of Prohibition.* New York: Oxford University Press, 2007. Presents ethical, religious, economic, psychological, and political arguments for cannabis policies that range from prohibition to unrestricted legalization.

Felbab-Brown, Vanda. *Shooting Up: Counterinsurgency and the War on Drugs.* Washington, DC: Brookings Institution, 2010. Argues that a laissez-faire policy toward illicit crop cultivation can reduce support for drug traffickers and increase cooperation with government intelligence gathering.

Fox, Steve, Paul Armentano, and Mason Tvert. *Marijuana Is Safer: So Why Are We Driving People to Drink?* White River Junction, VT: Chelsea Green, 2009. Compares and contrasts the relative harms and legal status of the two most popular recreational substances in the world—marijuana and alcohol.

Ghodse, Hamid, ed. *International Drug Control in the 21st Century.* Burlington, VT: Ashgate, 2008. Analyzes the ways in which different parts of the world have responded to the problems of drug use and dependence.

Gray, James P. *Why Our Drug Laws Have Failed and What We Can Do About It: A Judicial Indictment of the War on Drugs.* Philadelphia:

Temple University Press, 2012. Argues that a policy of drug prohibition has failed and contends that new options emphasizing education and treatment should prevail.

Grim, Ryan. *This Is Your Country on Drugs: The Secret History of Getting High in America.* Hoboken, NJ: Wiley, 2010. Traces the evolution of the long US relationship with drugs, commenting on the impact of antidrug policies.

Kuhn, Cynthia, Scott Swartzwelder, and Wilkie Wilson. *Buzzed: The Straight Facts About the Most Used and Abused Drugs from Alcohol to Ecstasy.* 3rd ed. New York: Norton, 2008. Relays information for understanding how drugs affect the body and behavior.

Lyman, Michael D. *Drugs in Society: Causes, Concepts, and Control.* 6th ed. Boston: Anderson, 2010. Analyzes the diverse perspectives on dealing with the impact of drug use and drug trafficking on American society.

Provine, Doris Marie. *Unequal Under Law: Race in the War on Drugs.* Chicago: University of Chicago Press, 2007. Traces the history of race in antidrug efforts, arguing that campaigns to criminalize drug use have always been racist.

Regan, Trish. *Joint Ventures: Inside America's Almost Legal Marijuana Industry.* Hoboken, NJ: Wiley, 2011. Explores the inner workings of America's exploding marijuana industry and its underground economy.

Reznicek, Michael J. *Blowing Smoke: Rethinking the War on Drugs Without Prohibition and Rehab.* Lanham, MD: Rowman and Littlefield, 2011. Argues against the disease model of drug addiction, favoring a habit model for handling addiction and for the legalization of all drugs.

Room, Robin, Benedikt Fischer, Wayne Hall, Simon Lenton, and Peter Reuter. *Cannabis Policy: Moving Beyond Stalemate.* New York: Oxford University Press, 2010. Reviews the health effects, trends in use, and legal stances on marijuana, exploring the impacts of various changes in policy.

Walker, Samuel. *Sense and Nonsense About Crime, Drugs, and Communities.* 7th ed. Belmont, CA: Wadsworth, 2011. Challenges common misconceptions about crime control, guns, and drugs, from both conservative and liberal propositions.

Periodicals and Internet Sources

Abramsky, Sasha. "The War Against the 'War on Drugs,'" *Nation*, July 6, 2009.

Armentano, Paul. "How to End Mexico's Deadly Drug War," *Freeman*, December 2009.

Balko, Radley. "The Drug War's Collateral Damage," *Reason*, January 23, 2009.

Bandow, Doug. "It's Time to Declare Peace in the War Against Drugs," *Forbes*, October 17, 2011.

Bennett, William J., Alexandra Datig, and Seth Leibsohn. "We Ignore Rise in Drug Abuse Among Kids," CNN.com, September 24, 2010. www.cnn.com.

Black, Conrad. "The Drug-War Failure," *National Review*, October 28, 2010.

Califano, Joseph A., Jr. and William J. Bennett. "Do We Really Want a Needle Park on American Soil?," *Wall Street Journal*, June 30, 2011.

Carden, Art. "Let's Be Blunt: It's Time to End the Drug War," *Forbes*, April 19, 2012.

Chapman, Steve. "How to Profit by Expanding Freedom," *Reason*, October 11, 2010.

Charen, Mona. "Where Ron Paul Is Right," *National Review*, December 2, 2011.

Christian Science Monitor. "Legalize Marijuana? Not So Fast," May 22, 2009.

Drum, Kevin. "A Patriot's Guide to Legislation," *Mother Jones*, July/August 2009.

Duke, Steven B. "Drugs: To Legalize or Not," *Wall Street Journal*, April 25, 2009.

DuPont, Robert L. "What's Wrong with Legalizing Illegal Drugs?," Institute for Behavior and Health, March 24, 2009. www.ibhinc.org.

Economist. "How to Stop the Drug Wars," March 7, 2009.

Espach, Ralph. "Should Central America Legalize Drugs?," *Atlantic*, February 28, 2012.

Fox, Steve. "Lies About Marijuana Drive People to a Much More Harmful Drug—Booze," *AlterNet*, November 9, 2009. www .alternet.org.

Friedersdorf, Conor. "Legalize Drugs Now," *Daily Beast*, October 23, 2009. www.thedailybeast.com.

Gupta, Sanjay. "Why I Would Vote No on Pot," *Time*, January 8, 2009.

Healy, Bernadine. "Legalize Marijuana? Obama Was Right to Say No," *U.S. News & World Report*, February 4, 2009.

Healy, Gene. "Time to Wind Down the War on Drugs," *DC Examiner*, December 1, 2009. www.washingtonexaminer.com.

Horton, Scott. "Is Reason Winning the War on Drugs?," *Harper's*, May 2010.

Kain, Erik. "A Victory Against the War on Drugs," *Mother Jones*, May 31, 2012.

Kleiman, Mark A.R., Jonathan P. Caulkins, and Angela Hawken. "Rethinking the War on Drugs," *Wall Street Journal*, April 22, 2012.

Kristof, Nicholas D. "End the War on Pot," *New York Times*, October 28, 2010.

Longmire, Sylvia. "Legalization Won't Kill the Cartels," *New York Times*, June 18, 2011.

Lynch, Tim. "Drug Czar Should Go," *Washington Times*, February 6, 2010.

Lynch, Tim, and Juan Carlos Hidalgo. "Get Serious About Decriminalizing Drugs; Others Are," *San Jose (CA) Mercury News*, September 29, 2009.

Mac Donald, Heather. "Is the Criminal-Justice System Racist?," *City Journal*, Spring 2008.

Mazurak, Zbigniew. "End the War on Drugs Now," *American Thinker*, March 26, 2011.

McWhorter, John. "End the Drug War, Mr. President," *New Republic*, March 10, 2012.

Mirken, Bruce. "The Case for Medical Marijuana," *Forbes*, August 21, 2009.

Miron, Jeffrey. "Making the Case for Marijuana Legalization," CNBC.com, April 20, 2012. www.cnbc.com.

Miron, Jeffrey A., and Katherine Waldock. "Making an Economic Case for Legalizing Drugs," *Philadelphia Inquirer,* October 3, 2010.

Moskos, Peter, and Stanford "Neill" Franklin. "Time to Legalize Drugs," *Washington Post,* August 17, 2009.

Nadelmann, Ethan. "The Forty-Year Quagmire: An Exit Strategy for the War on Drugs," *Nation,* June 17, 2011.

New York Times Upfront. "The Myth of 'Medical Marijuana,'" April 2, 2012.

Pacula, Rosalie Liccardo. "Legalizing Marijuana: Issues to Consider Before Reforming California State Law," Rand Corporation, October 2009. www.rand.org.

Parker, Kathleen. "Phelps Takes a Hit," *Washington Post,* February 4, 2009.

Power, Jonathan. "Legalizing Drugs the Only Answer," *Toronto Star,* August 11, 2010.

Saunders, Debra J. "Medicalization of America's Drug War," *San Francisco Chronicle,* April 19, 2012.

Singer-Vine, Jeremy. "A Toke and a Tax," *Slate,* June 10, 2009. www.slate.com.

Stossel, John. "End the Drug War," *Reason,* June 17, 2010.

Talvi, Silja J.A. "Ending the War on Drugs," *In These Times,* March 2009.

Walters, John P. "Drugs: To Legalize or Not," *Wall Street Journal,* April 25, 2009.

Western, Bruce. "Decriminalizing Poverty," *Nation,* December 27, 2010.

Wilkinson, Will. "I Smoke Pot, and I Like It," *Week,* April 2, 2009.

Will, George F. "Should the US Legalize Hard Drugs?," *Washington Post,* April 11, 2012.

Websites

Drug Enforcement Administration (www.justice.gov/dea). This website contains information on US drug policy and links to information about drugs.

Hemp and Cannabis Foundation (thc-foundation.com). This website of an organization that aims to help medical marijuana patients contains information about legal issues related to medical marijuana, medical marijuana clinics, and research on medical uses of marijuana.

Monitoring the Future (www.monitoringthefuture.org). This website contains information about an ongoing study of the behaviors and attitudes of American young people, including their behaviors and attitudes with respect to drug use.

Index

failure of initiatives for marijuana legalization in, 92

impact of marijuana legalization in, 70

Proposition 19 results in, *94*

California Medical Association, 102

Canada, failure of bill decriminalizing marijuana in, 102

Cantú, Silvano, 69, 71

Cardoso, Fernando Henrique, 98

Caulkins, Jonathan P., 52, 53, 56

Christian Science Monitor (newspaper), 91

Cocaine, 7

decline in use of, 11

prevalence of use of, 63

tons seized by US, *66*

Compassionate Use Act (CA, 1996), 79

Congressional Research Service, 59

Controlled Substances Act (CSA, 1970), 7, 79

Cortez, Edgar, 70

Criminal penalties, federal, 7

D

Davis, Artur, 40

De Jesús, José, 68

DEA. *See* Drug Enforcement Administration

Deaths

accidental, drug overdoses as leading cause of, 53

from alcohol, 103

from drug violence in Mexico, 60, 65, 70

Decriminalization, 8

benefits of, are overstated, 51–56

impact on US economy, 48

in Portugal, drug use before/after, *54*

trend toward, has failed, 21–25

Department of Health and Human Services, US (DHHS), 63

Dickinson, Elizabeth, 64

Drug courts, 41, 56, 60

Drug Enforcement Administration (DEA), 19, 61, 78, 84

creation of, 7

Drug prohibition

current laws on, should be repealed, 96–100

has failed, 26–31

Drugs and Drug Policy (Kleiman, Caulkins and Hawken), 52, 103

Dunbar, Pete, 95

E

Einstein, Albert, 47, 58, 88

W

Wall Street Journal (newspaper), 100

Walters, John P., 10, *13*

War on drugs
  has increased incarceration rates, 29
  has reduced drug problem, 10–15
  is destroying black America, 32–39
  is not cause of problems in poor communities, 40–44
  is not working, 16–20
  opinion on, 42, *99*
  origins of, 7, 18
  Ron Paul and, 46–50

Washington (state), approval of marijuana legalization in, 88

Wead, Doug, 46

Wente, Margaret, 101

Z

Zedillo, Ernesto, 98

Picture Credits

© AP Images, 87

© AP Images/J.Scott Applewhite, 47

© AP Images/Damian Dovarganes, 83

© AP Images/Armando Franca, 53

© AP Images/Eric Risberg, 103

© AP Images/Paul Sakuma, 94

© Yuri Cortez/AFP/Getty Images, 61

© David R. Frazier Photolibrary, Inc./Alamy, 45

© Kevork Djanezian/Getty Images, 30

© Gale, Cengage, 22, 29, 35, 49, 54, 66, 75, 89, 93, 99, 104

© Michael Karlsson/Alamy, 9, 36, 43

© Keystone/Getty Images, 17

© David Paul Morris/Bloomberg via Getty Images, 76

© Scott Olson/Getty images, 13

© STR/AFP/Getty Images, 69

© Justin Sullivan/Getty Images, 72

© Eric Thayer/Getty Images, 24

© Alex Wong/Getty Images, 97

2/15 ⊖ 10/14